Wastiary

Wastiary

A bestiary of waste

Edited by
Michael Hennessy Picard, Albert Brenchat-Aguilar,
Timothy Carroll, Jane Gilbert and Nicola Miller

First published in 2023 by
UCL Press
University College London
Gower Street
London WC1E 6BT

Available to download free: www.uclpress.co.uk

Collection © Editors, 2023
Text © Authors, 2023
Images © Authors and copyright holders named in captions, 2023

The authors have asserted their rights under the Copyright, Designs and Patents Act 1988 to be identified as authors of this work.

A CIP catalogue record for this book is available from The British Library.

This book contains third-party copyright material that is not covered by the book's Creative Commons licence. Details of the copyright ownership and permitted use of third-party material is given in the image (or extract) credit lines. If you would like to reuse any third-party material not covered by the book's Creative Commons licence, you will need to obtain permission directly from the copyright owner.

This book is published under a Creative Commons Attribution-Non-Commercial 4.0 International licence (CC BY-NC 4.0), https://creativecommons.org/licenses/by-nc/4.0/. This licence allows you to share, copy, distribute and transmit the work for personal and non-commercial use providing author and publisher attribution is clearly stated. If you wish to use the work commercially, use extracts or undertake translation you must seek permission from the authors. Attribution should include the following information:

Picard, M., Brenchat-Aguilar, A. Carroll, T., Gilbert, J. and Miller, N. (eds). 2023. *Wastiary: A bestiary of waste*. London: UCL Press. https://doi.org/10.14324/111.9781800085183

Further details about Creative Commons licences are available at http://creativecommons.org/licenses/

ISBN: 978-1-80008-520-6 (Hbk)
ISBN: 978-1-80008-519-0 (Pbk)
ISBN: 978-1-80008-518-3 (PDF)
ISBN: 978-1-80008-521-3 (epub)
DOI: https://doi.org/10.14324/111.9781800085183

Contents

List of figures vii
Notes on contributors xi
Foreword by Clare Melhuish and Nicola Miller xx

Introduction, by Michael Hennessy Picard, Albert Brenchat-Aguilar,
Timothy Carroll and Jane Gilbert 1

	for Strips of paper, by Nina Mathijsen	8
A	for Architecture of ruins, by Jonathan Hill	9
B	for Bomb ecologies, by Leah Zani	12
C	for Capitalism (plastic), by Amanda Boetzkes	15
D	for Data waste, by Roxana Vatanparast and Elettra Bietti	18
E	for Excrement, by Franziska Neumann	25
F	for Fire, by Stamatis Zografos	28
G	for Ground up, by Onya McCausland	32
H	for Hairs, by Robyn Adams	35
I	for Identity, by Caitlin DeSilvey	38
J	for Junk bonds, by David Sim	42
K	for Kinship (chemical), by Angeliki Balayannis	45
L	for Land waste, by Sonia Freire Trigo	49
M	for Microbes, by Elaine Cloutman-Green	53
N	for Nalu, by Melissa McCarthy	56
Ñ	for Ñiquiñaque/extraÑo, by Adriana Laura Massidda and Hanna Baumann	59
O	for Outsourcing, by Matthijs de Bruijne	63
P	for Problem, by Bruno Vindrola-Padrós and Ulrike Sommer	66

Q	for Queer liveliness/Queer matter/Queer toxin, by Mel Y. Chen	70
R	for Rubble, by Adam Przywara	72
S	for Space junk, by Alice Gorman	75
T	for Time and Tower: Grenfell, by José Torero Cullen	79
U	for Underground, by Luke Bennett	81
V	for Vastus, by Véra Ehrenstein	84
W	for Wasteland, by Miranda Griffin	87
X	for Xenophobia, by Huda Tayob	90
Y	for Yawning and Yearning, by Tatiana Thieme	93
Z	for Zero waste, by Pushpa Arabindoo	97
*	for Corona shapes, by Albert Brenchat-Aguilar	100
1	for 1%, by Andreas Philippopoulos-Mihalopoulos	106
2	for HS2, by Chia-Lin Chen	110
3	for From 3rd world to included 3rds, by Lucy Bell	114
4&6	for 4th Industrial Revolution and 6th extinction, by Everisto Benyera	119
5	for 5G, by Sy Taffel	122
7	for 7 dear things, by Maja and Reuben Fowkes	129
8	for Octopus, by Tina Beigi	132
9	for 9/11, by Michael Hennessy Picard	136

Epilogue, by Tamar Garb   140

Bibliography   145

List of figures

0.1	Vivan Sundaram, *Prospect*, 2008, archival pigment print, 104.5 × 59.5 inches, ed 5/10 (detail). © Vivan Sundaram. Courtesy of the artist.	xx
A.0	Nina Mathijsen, *Collage A*, 2021. © takeadetour.eu. Courtesy of the artist.	9
A.1	Giovanni Battista Piranesi, *Piazzale dei Cavalieri di Malta*, Rome, 1766. The enclosing wall with obelisks and monuments. Photograph, Izabela Wieczorek. Courtesy of the photographer.	11
B.0	Nina Mathijsen, *Collage B*, 2021. © takeadetour.eu. Courtesy of the artist.	12
B.1	Leah Zani, *Bomb Ecologies*, date unknown. Courtesy of the author.	14
C.0	Nina Mathijsen, *Collage C*, 2021. © takeadetour.eu. Courtesy of the artist.	15
C.1	Diana Lelonek, *Centre for Living Things*, 2016–. Courtesy of the artist.	16
D.0	Nina Mathijsen, *Collage D*, 2021. © takeadetour.eu. Courtesy of the artist.	18
D.1	Tom Ravenscroft, *TeleHouse North 2 at East India Dock campus*, 2016. Courtesy of the architect.	23
E.0	Nina Mathijsen, *Collage E*, 2021. © takeadetour.eu. Courtesy of the artist.	25
E.1	Isaac Cruikshank, *Indecency*, 1799. London: S.W. Fores. Photograph. © Library of Congress Prints and Photographs Division.	27

F.0	Nina Mathijsen, *Collage F*, 2021. © takeadetour.eu. Courtesy of the artist.	28
F.1	Rhona Eve Clews, *Coax*, 2018. Courtesy of the artist.	30
G.0	Nina Mathijsen, *Collage G*, 2021. © takeadetour.eu. Courtesy of the artist.	32
G.1	Six Bells Mine Water Treatment Scheme 51°43 33.56 N 3°07 58.63 W 638 m. ©2019 Google.	33
H.0	Nina Mathijsen, *Collage H*, 2021. © takeadetour.eu. Courtesy of the artist.	35
H.1	Pareid Architecture, *Follicle*, 2019. Courtesy of the architects.	36
I.0	Nina Mathijsen, *Collage I*, 2021. © takeadetour.eu. Courtesy of the artist.	38
I.1	Mellissa Fisher, *Microbial Me*, 2015. In collaboration with Professor Mark Clements and Dr Richard Harvey. Supported by ThermoFisher Scientific. Courtesy of the artist.	40
J.0	Nina Mathijsen, *Collage J*, 2021. © takeadetour.eu. Courtesy of the artist.	42
J.1	Hilary Powell and the Bank Job team, *Big Bang 2: Debt explosion*, 2019. Photograph by Graeme Truby.	43
K.0	Nina Mathijsen, *Collage K*, 2021. © takeadetour.eu. Courtesy of the artist.	45
K.1	Angeliki Balayannis, *SARPI-Veolia incinerator smoke stack, Dąbrowa Górnicza, Poland*, 2016. Courtesy of the author.	46
L.0	Nina Mathijsen, *Collage L*, 2021. © takeadetour.eu. Courtesy of the artist.	49
L.1	Hilary Powell, *The Games*, 2017. Courtesy of the artist.	50
L.2	Sonia Freire Trigo, *Activities on 'vacant' land in the Vauxhall Nine Elms Battersea Opportunity Area, London*, 2012. Courtesy of the author.	51
L.3	Sonia Freire Trigo, *Leftovers of the temporary uses of vacant land in the Royal Docks, London*, 2015. Courtesy of the author.	51
L.4	Sonia Freire Trigo, *Time suspended over the vacant land on Silvertown Quays, London*, 2015. Courtesy of the author.	52
M.0	Nina Mathijsen, *Collage M*, 2021. © takeadetour.eu. Courtesy of the artist.	53
M.1	Sonja Bäumel, *Microbial entanglement*, Frankfurter Kunstverein, 2019. Photograph: copyright Robert Schittko.	54
N.0	Nina Mathijsen, *Collage N*, 2021. © takeadetour.eu. Courtesy of the artist.	56

Ñ.0	Nina Mathijsen, *Collage Ñ*, 2021. © takeadetour.eu. Courtesy of the artist.	59
Ñ.1	Martín Oesterheld, still from *La multitud* (Buenos Aires, 2012). Courtesy of the director.	61
O.0	Nina Mathijsen, *Collage O*, 2021. © takeadetour.eu. Courtesy of the artist.	63
O.1	Matthijs de Bruijne, *Union of Cleaners FNV in Brussels*, 4 April 2014. Courtesy of the artist.	65
P.0	Nina Mathijsen, *Collage P*, 2021. © takeadetour.eu. Courtesy of the artist.	66
P.1	Bruno Vindrola-Padrós, *The everyday pottery sherds at the Early Neolithic Criș settlement of Tășnad Sere (Satu Mare, Romania)*, 26 July 2016. Courtesy of the author.	68
Q.0	Nina Mathijsen, *Collage Q*, 2021. © takeadetour.eu. Courtesy of the artist.	70
R.0	Nina Mathijsen, *Collage R*, 2021. © takeadetour.eu. Courtesy of the artist.	72
S.0	Nina Mathijsen, *Collage S*, 2021. © takeadetour.eu. Courtesy of the artist.	75
S.1	NASA, *Energy flash when a projectile launched at speeds up to 17,000 mph impacts a solid surface at the Hypervelocity Ballistic Range at NASA's Ames Research Centre*, Mountain View, California, 1963. Copyleft.	76
S.2	NASA, *Wind tunnel test of Saturn rocket model*, 1962. Copyleft.	77
T.0	Nina Mathijsen, *Collage T*, 2021. © takeadetour.eu. Courtesy of the artist.	79
U.0	Nina Mathijsen, *Collage U*, 2021. © takeadetour.eu. Courtesy of the artist.	81
U.1	Nicole Clouston, *Microbial growth in mud from Lake Ontario Portrait*, 2018. Courtesy of the artist.	82
V.0	Nina Mathijsen, *Collage V*, 2021. © takeadetour.eu. Courtesy of the artist.	84
W.0	Nina Mathijsen, *Collage W*, 2021. © takeadetour.eu. Courtesy of the artist.	87
W.1	*Perceval à la Recluserie*, Bibliothèque Nationale de France, BNF Richelieu Manuscrits Français 111, fol. 244v, Quête du saint Graal, France, Poitiers, XVe siècle. Courtesy Bibliothèque Nationale de France.	88
X.0	Nina Mathijsen, *Collage X*, 2021. © takeadetour.eu. Courtesy of the artist.	90

Y.0	Nina Mathijsen, *Collage Y*, 2021. © takeadetour.eu. Courtesy of the artist.	93
Z.0	Nina Mathijsen, *Collage Z*, 2021. © takeadetour.eu. Courtesy of the artist.	97
*.0	Nina Mathijsen, *Collage **, 2021. © takeadetour.eu. Courtesy of the artist.	100
*.1	Chus Martínez, *Corona Tales*, 2020; collage by Albert Brenchat-Aguilar. © Ana Domínguez. Courtesy of the artist.	102
*.2	Eduardo Navarro, *Untitled*, 2020; animation: Esther Hunziker (see https://espaciofronterizo.com/borderland/animated-skins-part1/). © Eduardo Navarro. Courtesy of the artist.	103
1.0	Nina Mathijsen, *Collage 1*, 2021. © takeadetour.eu. Courtesy of the artist.	106
1.1	Andreas Philippopoulos-Mihalopoulos, *Oceans of Eternity V: Contract unto extinction,* at K.U.K. gallery, Trondheim, Norway, on 6 September 2022. Photograph by Melchior Blum. Courtesy of the author.	108
2.0	Nina Mathijsen, *Collage 2*, 2021. © takeadetour.eu. Courtesy of the artist.	110
3.0	Nina Mathijsen, *Collage 3*, 2021. © takeadetour.eu. Courtesy of the artist.	114
3.1	*Cartonera books.* Photograph by Vassilis Korkas, 2016. Courtesy of the artist.	117
4/6.0	Nina Mathijsen, *Collage 4*, 2021. © takeadetour.eu. Courtesy of the artist.	119
5.0	Nina Mathijsen, *Collage 5*, 2021. © takeadetour.eu. Courtesy of the artist.	122
7.0	Nina Mathijsen, *Collage 7*, 2021. © takeadetour.eu. Courtesy of the artist.	129
8.0	Nina Mathijsen, *Collage 8*, 2021. © takeadetour.eu. Courtesy of the artist.	132
9.0	Nina Mathijsen, *Collage 9*, 2021. © takeadetour.eu. Courtesy of the artist.	136
ZZ.1	*Car park at the quarantine hotel*. Photograph by Tamar Garb, June 2021. Courtesy of the author.	141
ZZ.2	*Food at the quarantine hotel*. Photograph by Tamar Garb, June 2021. Courtesy of the author.	142
ZZ.3	*Accumulated water bottles at the quarantine hotel*. Photograph by Tamar Garb, June 2021. Courtesy of the author.	143

Notes on contributors

Robyn Adams is Senior Research Fellow at the Centre for Editing Lives and Letters (CELL) at UCL. Her research interests focus on the collection, use and transmission of books and manuscripts in the sixteenth and seventeenth centuries, with particular emphasis on their material properties.

Pushpa Arabindoo is Associate Professor in Geography & Urban Design at the Department of Geography. She is a codirector of UCL Urban Laboratory leading the priority research theme 'Wasteland'. She is also the co-convenor of the interdisciplinary MSc Urban Studies programme. Working mainly in the southern Indian city of Chennai, she conducts research that engages with the question of the urban from the viewpoint of nature using the filters of waste and water. More recently, she has been developing a conceptualisation of hinterland for a better understanding of the interactions between the urban and the Anthropocene. She has used a range of creative methodologies in these pursuits, including collaborations with a photographer and a playwright.

Angeliki Balayannis is Senior Lecturer in Human Geography at the University of Exeter. She specialises in the material politics of pollution and waste, interrogating how hazardous materials are governed, sensed and managed. She undertakes interdisciplinary collaborations with a range of publics, including regulators, activists, artists and waste workers.

Hanna Baumann is Senior Research Fellow at UCL's Institute for Global Prosperity. She is interested in the intersection of urban and global circulations of people and matter. Her current research examines the role of infrastructures and public services in shaping the urban citizenship of non-citizens.

Tina Beigi is a PhD researcher at McGill University and a member of Economics for the Anthropocene, a global research-to-action network. She previously worked as an environmental engineer in the Arctic to evaluate the ecological impact of mining waste in vulnerable regions. Her research interests lie in the intersection of ecological economics and political economy. Her current work focuses on the critique of so-called sustainable technologies through the gaze of ecological economics. In her recent coauthored publication 'A postcolonial history of accumulation by contamination in the Gulf', she traces waste legacies in the wars across the Persian Gulf.

Lucy Bell is Researcher in Spanish-American Literature at Sapienza, the University of Rome. Since obtaining her PhD in Latin American Studies at the University of Cambridge, she has published widely in the field, including a coauthored monograph, *Taking Form, Making Worlds: Cartonera publishers in Latin America* (University of Texas Press, 2022).

Luke Bennett is Associate Professor in the Department of the Natural & Built Environment, Sheffield Hallam University, UK. An environmental lawyer by background, since 2010 Luke has been probing the underground in works including *In the Ruins of the Cold War Bunker: Affect, materiality and meaning making* (Rowman & Littlefield, 2017).

Everisto Benyera is Professor of African Politics in the Department of Political Sciences at the University of South Africa in Pretoria, South Africa. He researches and publishes on community-based, non-state transitional justice, human rights, transitology and decoloniality. Everisto is the author of *The Failure of the International Criminal Court in Africa: Decolonising global justice* (Routledge, 2022).

Elettra Bietti is Assistant Professor of Law and Computer Science at Northeastern University. She was previously Joint Postdoctoral Fellow at the NYU School of Law and Cornell Tech. She recently completed a doctorate at Harvard Law School and her work is on the regulation of platforms and data from a privacy and antitrust law perspective.

Amanda Boetzkes is Professor of Contemporary Art History and Theory at the University of Guelph. She is the author of *Plastic Capitalism: Contemporary art and the drive to waste* (MIT Press, 2019) and *The Ethics of Earth Art* (University of Minnesota Press, 2010), and coeditor of *Heidegger and the Work of Art History* (Ashgate Publishing, 2014).

Albert Brenchat-Aguilar is Lecturer (Teaching) at The Bartlett School of Architecture, UCL. His publications include 'A burst of architectural plots', in *Architecture and Culture* (vol. 10, 2022), and the edited volume *As Hardly Found in the Art of Tropical Architecture*, forthcoming from the Architectural Association Press (2023). Previously he cocurated the public programme and publications of the Institute of Advanced Studies, UCL; edited the digital platform *Ceramic Architectures*; and worked as an architect in Bombas Gens Arts Centre.

Matthijs de Bruijne's artistic practice is often a result of political involvement, and has arisen in recent years in collaboration with trade unions and other labour organisations. In 2010 he was invited by the Dutch Union of Cleaners to help this workers' organisation visualise its messages in a clear manner and create an identity for this part of the working class in the Netherlands. Since 2019 he has been creating the union archive, which will be passed on to the International Institute of Social History in Amsterdam.

Dr Timothy Carroll is Principal Research Fellow in Anthropology at UCL. His current research investigates the way that materials such as the body and the environment are marshalled within the religious, political and social discourse of the global community of Orthodox Christian Churches. He is the author of *Orthodox Christian Material Culture: Of people and things in the making of heaven* (Routledge, 2018) and coauthor of *A Return to the Object: Alfred Gell, art, and social theory* (Routledge, 2021).

Chia-Lin Chen is Lecturer at the Department of Geography & Planning, University of Liverpool. She is interested in exploring the relationship between transport and territorial dynamism across different spatial scales, seeking potential solutions through strategic planning and governance. She has coauthored and coedited extensively on high-speed rail and territorial development.

Mel Y. Chen is Richard and Rhoda Goldman Distinguished Chair of Undergraduate and Interdisciplinary Studies and Associate Professor of Gender & Women's Studies at the University of California, Berkeley. Books include *Animacies: Biopolitics, racial mattering, and queer affect* (Duke University Press, 2012), *Intoxicated: Race, disability and chemical intimacies of empire* and the coedited *Crip Genealogies*, both forthcoming with Duke.

Elaine Cloutman-Green is a healthcare scientist working across UCL and Great Ormond Street Hospital. She works within Infection Prevention and Control but holds a special interest in microbes and the environment. In connection with this special interest, she has been working with the London Clinical Senate to explore how the NHS can introduce innovations in order to reduce its carbon footprint.

Caitlin DeSilvey is Professor of Cultural Geography at the University of Exeter's Cornwall campus, where she is Associate Director for Transdisciplinary Research in the Environment and Sustainability Institute. Her recent publications include *After Discourse: Things, affects, ethics* (coedited; Routledge, 2020) and *Heritage Futures: Comparative approaches to natural and cultural heritage practices* (coauthored; UCL Press, 2020).

Véra Ehrenstein is CNRS Researcher at the Centre d'étude des mouvements sociaux, École des hautes études en sciences sociales, in Paris, France. Véra is a sociologist who is interested in better understanding some of the relations between science, innovation and global policy in the face of climate change.

Maja and Reuben Fowkes are art historians, curators and codirectors of the Postsocialist Art Centre (PACT) at the Institute of Advanced Studies, UCL. Their publications include *Art and Climate Change* (Thames & Hudson, 2022), *Central and Eastern European Art Since 1950* (Thames & Hudson, 2020) and *Ilona Németh: Eastern Sugar* (Sternberg Press, 2021). Recent curatorial projects include the exhibitions Colliding Epistemes at Bozar Brussels (2022) and Potential Agrarianisms at Kunsthalle Bratislava (2021). Their research on the Socialist Anthropocene in the Visual Arts is supported by a UKRI Frontier Research grant (http://www.translocal.org).

Sonia Freire Trigo is a lecturer at The Bartlett School of Planning (UCL) and director of their MSc Urban Regeneration programme. Her research interests focus on urban redevelopment and urban regeneration processes, with attention to the politics of planning and its influence on concepts of urban change and land scarcity.

Tamar Garb is Professor of Art History at UCL. Publications include *Sisters of the Brush: Women's artistic culture in late nineteenth-century Paris* (Yale University Press, 1994), *Bodies of Modernity: Figure and flesh in fin-de-siècle France* (Thames and Hudson, 1998) and *The Painted Face: Portraits of women in France 1814–1914* (Yale University Press, 2007). She specialises in photography and contemporary art in and from southern Africa. Curatorial projects include *Figures and Fictions: Contemporary South African photography* (2011), *Distance and Desire: Encounters with the African archive* (2014), *Conversations in Letter and Lines: William Kentridge and Vivienne Koorland* (2016) and *Made Routes* (2019).

Jane Gilbert studied at Cambridge and (briefly) at the Courtauld Institute and has lectured at UCL since 1997. She works on French and English medieval literature and is interested especially in conversations between medieval literature and modern critical theory. Her recent publications include *Medieval French Literary Culture Abroad* (Oxford University Press, 2020); coauthored with William Burgwinkle and Simon Gaunt, this book emerged from the AHRC-funded project recorded at http://www.medievalfrancophone.ac.uk, which investigated how Old French literary texts and manuscripts were produced and circulated outside France, with a view to projecting a non-national history of French literature. Her current project is on Form in Translation: how literary form translates between French, English and Latin in medieval texts and manuscripts, how forms are laid out in manuscripts, and the affective, literary and philosophical consequences.

Alice Gorman is Associate Professor at Flinders University in Adelaide. She is an internationally recognised leader in the field of space archaeology and author of the award-winning book *Dr Space Junk vs the Universe: Archaeology and the future* (MIT Press, 2020). Her research focuses on the archaeology and heritage of space exploration, including space junk, planetary landing sites, off-earth mining and space habitats. In 2020, asteroid 551014 Gorman was named in her honour.

Miranda Griffin is Assistant Professor of Medieval French at the University of Cambridge, and a Fellow of Murray Edwards College.

She is the author of *The Object and the Cause in the Vulgate Cycle* (Legenda, 2005) and *Transforming Tales: Rewriting metamorphosis in medieval French literature* (Oxford University Press, 2015), as well as articles on a range of topics in medieval French literature.

Jonathan Hill is Professor of Architecture and Visual Theory at The Bartlett School of Architecture, UCL, where he directs the MPhil/PhD Architectural Design programme. Jonathan is the author of *The Illegal Architect* (Black Dog Publishing, 1998), *Actions of Architecture* (Routledge, 2003), *Immaterial Architecture* (Routledge, 2006), *Weather Architecture* (Routledge, 2012), *A Landscape of Architecture, History and Fiction* (Routledge, 2016) and *The Architecture of Ruins* (Routledge, 2019).

Adriana Laura Massidda is an architect and researcher at the University of Sheffield. Her most recent work focused on the environmental history of two UK housing estates built over former sewage farms, also engaging a project of landscape codesign with local residents. Earlier, she studied the socio-ecological transformations of urban space in twentieth-century Buenos Aires shantytowns.

Nina Mathijsen Together with art director Marnix de Klerk, Nina Mathijsen is founder and co-owner of Detour, an Utrecht-based studio for visual communication, social campaigning and design. Nina uses collage, drawing, aquarelle and embroidery to illustrate social campaigns, such as the Dutch Union of Cleaners' struggle to improve their conditions of employment.

Melissa McCarthy's *Sharks, Death, Surfers: An illustrated companion* was published by Sternberg Press in 2019. Her next book, *Photo, Phyto, Proto, Nitro*, from Sagging Meniscus, emerges in 2023. Shorter pieces have appeared in *The Exacting Clam, Full Stop, Public Domain Review, The Yellow Paper* and other publications. McCarthy's recent teaching and talks include appearances at Glasgow School of Art; Tate Modern, London; and the Volksbühne, Berlin. Her two radio series – *Melissa McCarthy's View from a Shark* and *The Slipping Forecast* – can be found, along with further material, at her website http://sharksillustrated.org.

Onya McCausland is an artist based in London and South Wales. She teaches painting at the Slade School of Fine Art where she also leads a visual reading group, Environment, Ecology, Sustainability.

Nicola Miller is Director of the Institute of Advanced Studies. She joined UCL in 1990, became Professor of Latin American History in 2007 and was Head of the Department of History from 2007 to 2012. Her research is focused on the intellectual, cultural, political and international history of the Americas, in comparative and transnational perspectives; and on nationalism and national identity, especially in the Americas. Her recent research has been on the history and politics of knowledge, especially *Republics of Knowledge* (Princeton University Press, 2020).

Franziska Neumann is Junior Professor of Early Modern History at the Technical University of Braunschweig. She was Joint Junior Research Fellow at the Institute of Advanced Studies of UCL and the German Historical Institute London for 2019/20. Her research interests include environmental history, urban history and the history of waste.

Andreas Philippopoulos-Mihalopoulos is an artist, legal theorist and fiction author. He works with performance art, photography and text, as well as sculpture and painting. He is Professor of Law & Theory at the University of Westminster, and Director of The Westminster Law & Theory Lab. His fiction includes *The Book of Water*, published in Greek (Thines, 2017) and English (Eris, 2022).

Michael Hennessy Picard teaches Waste Law at the University of Edinburgh School of Law. His research focuses on the transnational regulation of global waste objects, from the recycling of shipwrecks to the (mis)management of outer space debris.

Adam Przywara is a PhD candidate in the Manchester Architecture Research Group at the University of Manchester. He holds a Master of Arts degree in Architectural History from The Bartlett, UCL. His research concerns the materiality of ruins and metabolism of rubble in the history of twentieth-century architecture.

David Sim is Associate Professor in US History at UCL. He works on the history of US foreign relations and is especially interested in imperial and transnational approaches to the history of the nineteenth-century United States.

Ulrike Sommer is Senior Lecturer in European Prehistory at the UCL Institute of Archaeology. Her research interests include the Neolithisation of Europe, taphonomy and lithic technology. She is currently running a fieldwork project on the early Neolithic of northwestern Romania. She is coeditor of *The Oxford Handbook of Archaeological Theory* (Oxford University Press, 2021) and area editor for Eurasia for the *Encyclopedia of Archaeology* (2nd edition, edited by Thilo Rehren and Efthymia Nikita; Elsevier, forthcoming 2023).

Sy Taffel is Senior Lecturer in Media Studies and codirector of the Political Ecology Research Centre at Massey University, Aotearoa-New Zealand. He is the author of *Digital Media Ecologies* (Bloomsbury, 2019). His research focuses on digital technology and the environment, digital media and society, automation, and digital labour.

Huda Tayob is currently a lecturer in Architectural Studies at the University of Manchester. She has previously taught at the University of Cape Town the Graduate School of Architecture, University of Johannesburg, and The Bartlett School of Architecture. She is a Mellon Fellow on the Canadian Centre for Architecture project Centring Africa. Her research focuses on minor, migrant and subaltern architectures, centred on the African continent and Global South. She is cocurator of the open access curriculum Race Space & Architecture (http://racespacearchitecture.org), and lead curator and project manager of the digital exhibition Archive of Forgetfulness (http://archiveofforgetfulness.com).

Tatiana A. Thieme is Associate Professor in Geography at UCL. Tatiana's contribution to this volume draws on ethnographic research conducted in Paris for a multi-sited collaborative project with Eszter Kovacs and Kavita Ramakrishnan, titled 'Temporary migrants or new European citizens? Geographies of integration and response between "camps" and the city' and funded by the British Academy's UK International Challenges award.

José Torero Cullen is Professor of Civil Engineering and Head of the Department of Civil, Environmental and Geomatic Engineering at UCL. He works in safety, remediation and sanitation, where he specialises in complex environments. He is a fellow of the Royal Academy of Engineering and the Royal Society of Edinburgh.

Roxana Vatanparast is an interdisciplinary legal scholar interested in technology, international law and digital global governance. She is currently a Fellow with the Transatlantic Technology Law Forum at

Stanford Law School. She holds a JD from UC Hastings (UC Law SF) and a PhD in Law & Institutions from the University of Turin.

Bruno Vindrola-Padrós is a Research Fellow for the ERC-funded project 'XSCAPE: Material Minds' at Christian-Albrechts-Universität (Kiel, Germany). He completed his doctoral studies at UCL Institute of Archaeology in 2021. His research focuses on how broken objects, and much of what we call waste today, shaped human practices during the European Neolithic, and how these human–material interactions enabled a different form of knowledge construction.

Leah Zani is a public anthropologist and poet writing on the cultural impact of war. Zani is the author of *Bomb Children* (Duke University Press, 2019) and *Strike Patterns* (Redwood Press, 2022). From 2018 to 2021, Zani was the poetry editor for the journal *Anthropology and Humanism*.

Stamatis Zografos is Lecturer (Teaching) in Architectural History and Theory at UCL's Bartlett School of Architecture. He is also the cofounder of Incandescent Square, an interdisciplinary platform for research and design with interests spanning from architecture and urbanism to critical heritage and curating. He is the author of *Architecture and Fire: A psychoanalytic approach to conservation*, published in 2019 by UCL Press.

Foreword

Figure 0.1 Vivan Sundaram, *Prospect*, 2008, archival pigment print, 104.5 × 59.5 inches, ed 5/10 (detail). © Vivan Sundaram. Courtesy of the artist.

Clare Melhuish, Director, UCL Urban Laboratory

For our first ever annual theme in 2019–20, UCL Urban Laboratory embraced a collaboration with the UCL Institute of Advanced Studies (IAS) in order to interrogate the idea of 'Waste' across the arts, humanities and social sciences, bringing urbanists, planners, architects, engineers, scientists and medics into the conversation with us. Launching the theme in October 2019, Tamar Garb, then Director of IAS, and I presented the first UCL public lecture by the Dean of The Bartlett and Professor of Urban Studies, Christoph Lindner, on the subject of his book *Global Garbage: Urban imaginaries of waste* (Routledge, 2015), with a response from Jose Torero Cullen (UCL Civil, Environmental and Geomatic Engineering), bringing perspectives from engineering to the discussion. Several rounds of funding for events and research proposals related to the theme were launched during the course of the year, emphasising the scope for the widest possible interpretation, and the need to think across or even bypass entrenched or established modes of thinking.

The opportunity to collaborate with IAS opened up a wide field of discussion across temporal, spatial and conceptual dimensions. But of course, the challenges and opportunities posed by Waste are central to the concerns of urbanists involved in planning, designing and managing cities and urban life, and particularly in the discourses around the circular economy and sustainability which have been driving innovation in urban thinking for many decades. These are explicitly represented in one of Urban Lab's priority research areas, Wasteland, while the Waste theme provided the focus for the Urban Practices module of our cross-disciplinary MSc Urban Studies programme, including an opportunity to work with the West End Partnership on issues around waste and urban management in London's West End. We also ran an open Waste photo competition, won by Tom Farshi from UCL Computer Science with an image titled 'Nocturnal Demolition'. As the judges noted, it focused attention on the waste generated by building demolition and replacement, and the intricate processes of sorting different waste and reusable components which it involves. It also represented night as a time of urban cleaning, maintenance and violent dismantling of the urban fabric: 'wasting' as process and action, not simply the end product we identify as 'waste'.

Sadly, due to the unanticipated arrival of COVID-19 in Spring 2020, many of the exciting proposals we funded were not able to take place. However, we are delighted that the *Wastiary* has provided such an engaging format in which to bring together and share with a wide cross-disciplinary audience so many of the valuable and thought-provoking ideas which the theme elicited during a difficult year. We anticipate that these contributions will fuel discussion around this challenging theme for many years to come, pushing the boundaries in how we think through and ultimately discard 'waste' as a redundant concept in the near future.

Nicola Miller, Director, UCL Institute of Advanced Studies

The first big project I heard about as incoming Director of IAS was the *Wastiary*, which was proposed by Albert Brenchat-Aguilar and Michael Picard in Summer 2020. Their marvellous idea immediately reassured me that my new role still promised to be intellectually invigorating, even though pandemic conditions were a bleak prospect for a cross-disciplinary institute that thrived on the potential for the unexpected and the revelatory created by *presence*. Over two years later, we now know that the experiences of lockdown and social distancing yielded many inventive adaptations to sustain intellectual conversations across boundaries, although none came without a cost. In this case, the fact that the programme of research and events that IAS and Urban Lab had co-funded could not take place meant that there was insufficient material for the planned publication of an issue on Waste for the IAS review *Think Pieces*. It was in this difficult context that Albert and Michael came up with the idea for the *Wastiary*.

The *Wastiary* was conceived as an illustrated volume of short contributions by researchers from across the arts, humanities and social sciences, reflecting from their various disciplines and perspectives upon the multiple meanings and manifestations of waste. The echo of a bestiary resonates in various ways discussed in the Introduction, but most vividly the 'beast' evokes how waste cannot be tamed, confined or managed. A strong visual emphasis was central to the original conception of the *Wastiary*, and we were delighted and privileged that artist Nina Mathijsen was able to work with us on the illustrations and design, partly funded by the IAS project 'New (Normal) Materialist Decay' supported by the Embassy of the Kingdom of the Netherlands. Without her beautiful drawings, the *Wastiary* would not only have been less attractive as a material object, but also far less effective in achieving its aim of stimulating readers to engage their imaginations as well as their intellects in addressing this most urgent phenomenon of our times.

We are proud to say that the editorial work was done collectively by Albert Brenchat-Aguilar, Timothy Carroll, Jane Gilbert, Nicola Miller and Michael Picard. After Michael and Albert had presented their idea, the whole team, plus Tamar Garb (who was then Director of the IAS), Jordan Rowe (Programme Manager of the Urban Lab) and Nicola Baldwin (Creative Fellow at the IAS), spent several weeks brainstorming for potential entries and contributors, from which pool a selection was made. Special mention is due to Tamar for her support in getting the project off the ground and for her continuing interest, not least as a contributor. We also appreciate the support of Clare Melhuish as Director of Urban Lab, the IAS's partner in the theme of Waste. Invaluable help with production was given at different stages by Marthe Lisson, Patricia Mascarell Llombart and Catherine Stokes. We would also like to thank Tim Mathews, academic editor at UCL Press, and Chris Penfold, commissioning editor, for their readiness to support this experimental publishing venture. Our wonderful contributors have borne with us through the long months of a publishing schedule; we warmly thank them for their readiness to engage with the project and their good-natured patience as it came to fruition. We reassure readers that all research in this volume was carried out in accordance with the highest standards of ethical review.

We hope that the wide variety of disciplinary approaches, together with the emphasis on storytelling as a research tool, opens up routes to new ways of seeing for both experts and novices. The *Wastiary* is not meant to be read straight through. The Introduction suggests some thematic connections to help get you started, but the book is an invitation to serendipity and to the lost pleasures of getting lost. Some things may jar; others may unexpectedly align, but we trust that some turns of the kaleidoscope will settle into new patterns that make meaning.

Introduction

Michael Hennessy Picard, Albert Brenchat-Aguilar, Timothy Carroll and Jane Gilbert

What is a 'wastiary'? One could regard it as a bestiary of waste, a heterodox compendium of jarring objects, creatures and artwork. The series of entries included here charts, in a playful and sometimes serendipitous way, the variety of themes and connections between disciplines on the uncomfortable but pressing topic of waste.

The *Wastiary* as a form of storytelling

Discards are in a permanent process of circulation and conversion. Identifying waste is therefore a constant challenge, which may blur the categories of cleanness and dirt, order and anarchy, norm and deviance, affluence and effluence. Discard studies, an emerging field of study addressing waste regimes and systems, aims to interrupt popular, intuitive, expected and common narratives about waste and wasting from various disciplinary standpoints.[1] Instead of 'why don't people recycle more?', discard studies asks 1) why is recycling considered appropriate in the first place, 2) how are recycling policies framed to make some (post-consumer) waste perceptible and other types of (industrial) waste invisible and 3) what must be discarded for such a system of recycling to persist?[2]

While the *Wastiary* emulates discard studies by addressing a range of cases across disciplines, it also makes use of storytelling as a heuristic method for understanding complex waste streams.[3] The *Wastiary* tells stories of waste-as-beast 'running out of control' as a core cognitive tool. As a mirror to the topic of waste, storytelling-as-research embraces the messiness and recursive process of stories and storytelling, of human entanglement with the world. It engages the reader's memory and imagination, opening up other sorts of knowledge and diverse kinds of action.

Since waste 'always overflows its official meanings, and the technical systems designed to manage and contain it',[4] one way to 'capture' it is by personifying it. The *Wastiary*'s 'zoomorphism' – its assignment of beastly characteristics to waste objects – and the short, incisive alphabetical and numerical entries are designed to help the reader process information in unexpected ways. The wide-ranging contributions offer critical insight into neglected aspects of waste systems. The *Wastiary* format also highlights the abnormality and absurdity of waste management practices. It increases our perception of waste by exaggerating its attributes until they become hyperbolic and fantastical. Complementing each entry, and following in the visual tradition of medieval bestiary, are montage illuminations for each initial. These original pieces, by Nina Mathijsen, play in the space between a high and venerable tradition of manuscripts and the discarded waste materials from which she has made the illuminations. The work of making waste visible – and the social and economic means by which waste is moved – is itself a political act.[5]

Furthermore, the visual element, and the format and presentation of the *Wastiary* as an aesthetic object, allow the entries and illustrations to be 'fresh sources of guidance and illumination', as revisiting the images, the entries and the whole volume may trigger new ways of thinking about a topic already well known.[6] As we begin to map out in the following sections, there are many ways to read the *Wastiary*. There are likewise many ways to peruse, thumb through and engage with the images. Together, the interplays of word and image, of waste as topic and waste as material for new designs, allow for what is strange, at the margin, often excluded and voiceless, to take centre stage. In this way, the *Wastiary*'s storytelling serves multiple purposes. It helps readers recognise waste systems and introduces discard studies' modes of critical thinking into the stories themselves.

Identifying waste

Considering the multiform beasts of waste allows us to highlight their often elusive, ambiguous character, and to muddy reductive binaries. The *Wastiary* brings together as beings of waste abandoned objects (A for Architecture of ruins, R for Rubble) and abandoned subjects

(Y for Yawning and Yearning). It insists on an inquisitiveness that incites closer inspection: what is generally perceived as an abandoned space may be occupied by people, plants and animals for whom it is valuable (L for Land waste); and what a dominant culture considers valuable and normal can often be toxic for marginalised groups (X for Xenophobia, Q for Queer liveliness/Queer matter/Queer toxin, * for Corona shapes). Without any claim to exhaustiveness, the *Wastiary* tries to give a voice to 'overlooked' or 'abandoned' social groups, who struggle in increasingly exhausted ecologies against inhuman labour conditions and hegemonic knowledge production (3 for From 3rd world to included 3rds, 1 for 1%, 4&6 for 4th Industrial Revolution and 6th extinction). The concept of waste emerges here as relative to class, race, gender and other intersections.

This collection also probes a more intimate relationship to discards (I for Identity). Since all humans are beasts of waste, we inscribe waste in our mental and bibliographic record, allowing the passing of time to recall memories, dreams and experiences that would otherwise have been forgotten. Waste intimacies bring buried emotions to the surface and offer the possibility to mourn and heal with objects 'belonging' to the past. Waste recovery can therefore mean more than recycling: it can be psychologically restorative. Drawing attention to the vulnerabilities of being situated in fragile environments, the *Wastiary*'s narratives operate as a form of ecological consciousness, rearranging the perception of what constitutes waste and value in our social imaginary (5 for 5G, J for Junk bonds, E for Excrement).

The ubiquity of waste

The *Wastiary* navigates the porous border between the many visible and invisible beasts of waste that compose or have shaped our reality. Visible beasts burn towers to the ground (T for Time and Tower: Grenfell; 9 for 9/11); they pile up like tabloids on a public train bench (O for Outsource) or run through the land at high speeds (2 for HS2). Invisible beasts surround us and, to some extent, are within us, composing us. They proliferate in the form of bacteria (M for Microbes), surf endlessly on waves of microplastic debris (C for Capitalism (plastic)) or creep surreptitiously out of the ground (G for Ground up, B for Bomb ecologies).

Whether visible or invisible to the naked eye, waste is ubiquitous: it accumulates vertically and evacuates horizontally. The vertical dimension is symbolised by the solemn chimneys of our modern cathedrals of production, as unholy smoke reaches the sky (C for Capitalism (plastic)). Still 'higher' technologies are represented by the space rocket, which comes crashing down to earth unexpectedly, or by the graveyard of disconnected satellites forming a ring around the globe (S for Space junk, D for Data waste). On the horizontal plane, toxic waste flows like blood through the veins of the world (P for Problem). It floats in water from the Arctic to the equator. It travels on land from the metropolis to the periphery and vice versa. Urban sprawl creates a new generation of 'smart' landfills monitored by sensors and spritzed with odour-neutralising perfume, while former dumping sites are converted to urban amenities such as parks, homes and stores, where hazards continue to spread unabated (Ñ for Ñiquiñaque).

Format and structure of the book

The book is structured around themes prompted by each letter of the alphabet and the numbers 1 to 9, along with some other heterogeneous graphic symbols: an arrangement which allows us to exhibit a diversity of resourceful and critical insights. From human DNA found in old books (H for Hairs) to the spread of cheap things under global capitalism (7 for 7 dear things), the *Wastiary* recounts stories of discard legacies on multiple scales – from the local archives to the global sweatshop, with no intended hierarchy of importance.

The *Wastiary*'s organisation in accordance with alphabetic and numeric conventions highlights such conventions' arbitrariness and allows for serendipitous encounters. When read in alphabetical order, 'A for Architecture of ruin' and 'B for Bomb ecologies' suggest to the reader creative ways to live with the broken form as a remnant of the past. Between 'B for Bomb ecologies' and 'C for Capitalism (plastic)', the common thread of oil as fuelling warfare and mass production can be traced. Equally fruitful connections can be produced by leaping back and forth between letters and numbers. A diagonal reading of 'Architecture of ruins', 'Fire', 'Rubble', 'Time and Tower' and '9/11' sketches a typology of vestiges.[7] A first distinction can be drawn between *ruins* and *rubble*, which serve alternative aims and operate on different timescales. In post-bellum Warsaw, rubble was quickly repurposed and grafted onto reconstruction efforts. In contrast, ruins are preserved and memorialised to remind, warn and advise about the past, present and future. A second distinction can be drawn between the emerging properties of ruin and rubble – their elevation into the urban space – and the undefined or imperceptible properties of *debris*. Ruin and rubble form part of the urban grid, whereas debris disappears out of sight. Once the fire had consumed Grenfell Towers and the Twin Towers, the remaining debris was either stored in bags under flats close to the incident in London or landfilled in Staten Island as unfit for repurposing.

Other kinds of thread, too, generate new insights. The same expression, 'a waste of time', occurring in different entries highlights the contrasting perspectives on waste depending on a subject's standpoint: a waste of time is positive when surfing on a beach (N for Nalu) but negative when stranded on a bench (Y for Yawning and Yearning). The *Wastiary* format invites the reader to 'make kin' (K for Kinship) using a heterodox toolbox, to draw together many threads of knowledge in an open-ended way.

The *Wastiary* is a repository, not a dictionary

The *Wastiary* does not provide a stable taxonomy, nor an exhaustive encyclopedia, nor a set of definitions: it rather gestures towards alternative framings of relationships with what humans (think that they) leave behind. Discards are strange, abandoned animals that come back into our lives transformed. We find this strange familiarity in premodern bestiaries, where 'real' animal species – including 'man' – were adorned with supernatural features, thus situating earthly times and tides relative to meanings and values that were conceived on a much larger scale, linking microcosm to macrocosm. (For a sumptuously illustrated Latin bestiary with modern English translation, see https://www.abdn.ac.uk/bestiary/. There is a lengthy discussion of human nature, body parts and ages on ff. 80v–93v.)

A bestiary is a repository of fantasies from a specific time and place, a literary form that was particularly popular in Europe in the Middle Ages. Similarly, the *Wastiary* is a 'menagerie' of our present-day mythologies ('circular economy'), crusades ('net zero waste') and legends about recycling and repurposing ('the little things that make a big difference'). One theme explored here is the nauseating repetition of history. The ancient format of the bestiary is used as a heuristic device to underscore modernity's recycling of old ideas and formulas. Promises of progress and redemption emerge as a historical pattern (V for Vastus). Nostalgic references to 'nature' re-emerge in attempts to popularise transitions to 'renewable energy'. Apocalypticism too has a long pedigree: there is no purity, there is no 'clean' energy, nor any reasonable formula for 'zero carbon emission' (Z for Zero waste). Recently, lithium-ion batteries – once hailed as essential components of a Green New Deal – have been identified as the cause of fires at landfills and waste treatment facilities. In other words, new sources of energy reproduce old waste management problems. The Wasteland, as an outcome of questions unasked, routes untaken and sicknesses unhealed, has haunted us since at least the twelfth century; but this historical recycling points also to opportunities (W for Wasteland).

The bestiary format is used here to conduct a 'natural history' of waste and describe the characteristics and the behaviours of 'waste specimens'. The neologism 'wastiary' combines the terms 'waste' and 'bestiary', since waste has acquired the animated qualities and features of a beast. The 'beast' in waste is what cannot be domesticated. Waste is beastly because of its emerging properties: the assemblage of waste and living things develops, over time, dynamic properties that go beyond the sum of its parts. In a world colonised by trash, there is a compelling dynamic of self-reproduction through self-destruction in the phenomenology of waste (F for Fire). In Catalonia, manure self-ignites under the scorching sun. A combination of high temperatures, moisture and air turns chicken dung into incendiary bombs, destroying crops, forests and the manure-producing animals themselves.

'Wastiary' further emphasises that waste is now behaving like an invasive species. Similarly to invasive species, waste systems can have 'agency' without having developed consciousness. For example, earth materials have degraded into space to such an extent that orbital space debris has now formed an ecosystem or colony of swarming metallic insects communicating back to earth long after their decommissioning (S for Space junk). The *Wastiary* presents a range of types of animated waste, which act as tricksters corrupting their initial design with unforeseen behaviour.

The phenomenology of waste still begs to be recognised a decade after the publication of Jane Bennett's *Vibrant Matter*.[8] In it, Bennett argued that garbage hills are 'actants', alive with toxins seeping into the ground and bubbling into the air, where vital materiality is in self-alteration, as it continues its activities long after having been discarded. As garbage mutates, it becomes discordant with its previous self and involved in new sets of relations or 'assemblage'. Dimensions of biological existence (breathe, eat, swim, ingest, digest, release) are rearranged around *para*-sites of civilisation (U for Underground). New York subway rats mutate their genetic composition by ingesting heavy toxic metals, while storks modify their migration patterns to gorge on 'junk food' in municipal landfills. On the seabed, octopi convert human debris into shelters and weapons (8 for Octopus). Toxic substances reduce human sperm count and affect reproduction rates, while waste pollution on Mars anticipates future colonisation. Junk here posits itself a priori – in the foreground of evolution – rather than a posteriori. Waste ecologies subvert the supposed natural order, reminding us that superfluity precedes necessity, and that life on earth began with an erotic show of toxic gases intertwined in an opening dance.[9]

Notes

1 Zsuzsa Gille & Josh Lepawsky, eds, *The Routledge Handbook of Waste Studies* (Routledge, 2021).
2 Max Liboiron & Josh Lepawsky, *Discard Studies: Wasting, systems, and power* (MIT Press, 2022), p. 3.
3 Patrick John Lewis & Katia Hildebrandt, *Storytelling as Qualitative Research* (SAGE Publications Limited, 2020).
4 Lewis & Hildebrandt, *Storytelling as Qualitative Research*, p. 2.
5 Michael Thompson, *Rubbish Theory: The creation and destruction of value* (Oxford University Press, 1979).
6 Robert Farris Thompson, 'The aesthetics of the cool', *African Arts* 7:1 (1973), pp. 40–91.
7 Alain Schnapp, *Une histoire universelle des ruines* (Seuil, 2020).
8 Jane Bennett, *Vibrant Matter: A political ecology of things* (Duke University Press, 2010).
9 Michel De Broin, *Molysmocène*, Video projection on the façade of Théâtre Maisonneuve, Montreal, 2015.

Strips of paper

Nina Mathijsen

Back in the day, one of my first typography classes in art school that blew my mind – almost two decades ago – was about the white space around, in between and inside letters. The pieces of space that unnoticeably guide your eyes, make a letter stand out, form the invisible foundation of the letter itself. It makes language readable, and for most people (non-designers mostly) it is the white that is overlooked, unnoticed, unidentified. But it has an essential function for the reader. It is the silence in a piece of music. The passe-partout around a painting. It binds, gives atmosphere and can cause feelings of relaxation or suffocation for the eye of the beholder (designers mostly).

Since my childhood I have been fascinated by the overlooked. The colour numbering indication on the sides of printed fabric, functional lettering in the selvage of woven fabric, back sides of embroidery, but also: people that live in the social periphery of society, the less privileged and less visible. The single socks on the pavement (I still don't understand this phenomenon). The beauty of faded dead tulips. 'Forgotten' vegetables. Pieces of ceramic which I found everywhere and turn into mosaics. And: the huge jungle of scraps, which I collected to make collages.

For this *Wastiary*, I used those scraps. I also used the back sides of non-scraps: pieces of Pictures that were Precious and I kept for a Special Occasion. Now I just turned them upside down uncompromised because I needed this specific random strip of colour or shape in one of the initials. Also, during the development of these collages, I tore, ripped and cut but left the residue of this process. Normally I would either work with the care and precision of a surgeon; or Photoshop, erase, clean, remove, hide those torn pieces of paper, rough edges and cuts and messy blobs of glue. Now I just let them be there. Because it is about them.

Architecture of ruins

Jonathan Hill

Figure A.0   Nina Mathijsen, *Collage A*, 2021. © takeadetour.eu. Courtesy of the artist.

Many societies have conceived buildings as solidly stable and resistant to the weather, nature and time. In this schema, a ruin is understood only in terms of loss, failure, destruction and decay. However, there is an alternative and significant history of architecture, in which a building is designed, occupied and imagined as a ruin. This design practice and ethos, which we may term an 'architecture of ruins', conceives of a monument and a ruin as creative, interdependent and simultaneous themes within a single building dialectic. It addresses temporal and environmental questions in poetic, psychological and practical terms, and stimulates questions of personal and collective identities, nature and culture, weather and climate, permanence and impermanence, and life and death. As the etymology of the term derives from Latin *monēre*, meaning to remind, warn and advise, a monument's purpose is complex and challenging, and not merely commemorative, while the ruin is a temporal metaphor representing potential as well as loss, and also an environmental model combining nature and culture. Considering a building as a dialogue between a monument and a ruin intensifies the already blurred relations between the constructed, unfinished and decayed, and envisages the past, present and future in a single architecture.

Like building sites, ruins are full of potential. In revealing not only what is lost, but also what is incomplete, a ruin suggests the future as well as the past. As a stimulus to the imagination, a ruin's incomplete and broken forms expand architecture's allegorical and metaphorical capacity, indicating that a building can remain unfinished, literally and in the imagination, focusing attention on the creativity of users as well as architects.

Assembled from materials of diverse ages, from the newly formed to those centuries or millions of years old, and incorporating varied states of transformation and decay, a building is a time machine. Design, construction, maintenance and ruination may occur simultaneously, fluctuating according to specific spaces and components. Ruination does not only occur once a building is without a function. Instead, it is a continuing process that develops at differing speeds in differing spaces while a building is occupied. Accommodating partial ruination, focused repair and selective reuse can question the recurring cycles of production, obsolescence and waste that feed consumption in a capitalist society.

The dangers of global warming are real and need to be addressed when and where possible, notably because their effects are unequal, often causing greater harm to poorer, powerless communities.

Figure A.1 Giovanni Battista Piranesi, *Piazzale dei Cavalieri di Malta*, Rome, 1766. The enclosing wall with obelisks and monuments. Photograph, Izabela Wieczorek. Courtesy of the photographer.

But greater awareness of climate change may encourage cultural, social and environmental innovations and benefits, whether at a local or regional scale, including greater appreciation of the Earth and criticism of the isolationist policies of corporations and nations. A building designed, occupied and imagined as a ruin acknowledges the coproduction of multiple authors – human and non-human – and is an appropriate model for architecture in an era of increasing climate change.

Bomb ecologies

Leah Zani

Figure B.0 Nina Mathijsen, *Collage B*, 2021. © takeadetour.eu. Courtesy of the artist.

The stroke of the politician's pen may end the war, but it cannot clear the minefield, and so we must add a familiar ecology to our compendium of waste. This ecology, seeded by the soldier, has become more far-reaching in its effects within the last century. I call these places *bomb ecologies*. These are zones where warfare and military waste have a sustained impact on the conditions of life, slowly eroding distinctions between geopolitics and the environment. Societies and environments are degraded by military waste such as cluster munitions, land mines and chemical agents; abandoned equipment such as tanks, ships and gun installations; and militarised places such as razed towns, discarded army bases, weapons factories and toxic dumps. These weapons, equipment and places shape everyday life for generations after wars end.

In upland Laos, locals build their villages out of military waste: houses built on foundations of emptied bombs, craters turned into fisheries. They call these places 'bomb villages' (*ban labaerd*), a phrase that refers both to these villages being targets of US airstrikes from the 1960s–70s and to recent village reconstruction out of debris. When I began my fieldwork, I thought the phrase morbid, but later recognised the dignity of building a life out of waste. In a farmer's harvest shed, I found sheafs of garlic bundled on top of a neat row of artillery cartridges, both kept for future domestic use. I would have mistaken them for firewood if I hadn't been looking properly. The foundation plinths of the shed were also made of cartridges, half-buried and nearly unrecognisable. The farmer harvested the bombs from the same field as the garlic. It is this power to secretly transform the everyday that gives bomb ecologies their unnerving surreality: extremely difficult to identify at first, and then impossible to ignore. New grasslands filled the empty, blighted forests around the village – and, as a Lao interlocutor told me, bombs were 'like snakes in the grass'. This ecology is felt before it is seen: fear, hope and paranoia are its native beasts.

A half-century after the US airstrikes, ongoing military wasting provokes new ways of living that are not dependent on military plans or subservient to geopolitical claims. War and peace are not significant coordinates for mapping bomb ecologies. Rather, the relevant coordinates are explosivity, militarisation, adaptation and resilience. Explosivity has its own generative powers, and new forms of ecological and social life develop in the craters and on the denuded hillsides of ageing battlefields. Engaging with war as ecological waste opens the possibility for treating bombs as something other

Figure B.1 Leah Zani, *Bomb Ecologies*, date unknown. Courtesy of the author.

than weapons – foundation plinths, fenceposts, fisheries, cooking pots, snakes. These lived ruins invite a scholarship that transcends war. This move – away from war, towards the possibilities of everyday life – is the sorrow and hope of bomb ecologies.

Capitalism (plastic)

Amanda Boetzkes

Figure C.0   Nina Mathijsen, *Collage C*, 2021. © takeadetour.eu. Courtesy of the artist.

The spreading topology of plastic appears as both an extension, and an often invisible intensification, of capitalism's wasting of planetary life. Plastic is a petroleum-based material that was chemically refined over the post-war decades for its flexibility and easy disposability. Now it spreads as the monstrous urform of waste capitalism. In its resistance to biodegradation, plastic has penetrated the 'web of life'[1] on every scale. As a solid waste, it accumulates in waterways. In its microscopic form, it is disseminated throughout the world's oceans and weather systems. It causes chemical changes in the air and genetic changes in animals. It has fused with the Earth's geostrata, becoming a key marker horizon of the

Anthropocene. It is not merely an inert pollution, but rather a vital form that expresses and perpetuates capitalism's capacity to affect anthropogenesis and glean profit through its waste. Plastic is a fantastic beast of the capitalist oil ecology insofar as it behaves as both a cause and an effect of the drive to waste. Further, it expands the temporal and spatial scales of capitalism's planetary bearing. Plastic is now the antithesis of disposability; it is a vector of capitalism's expansion in and through the economy's ingestion of waste.

With the plastic predicament, in which our sense of the environment has been mediated by plastic, the question remains: what kind of critical gesture can be made from within its totalising infiltration of life? Contemporary art stages the ambiguity between plastic forms and biological life, demonstrating how the philosophical ideal of plasticity itself – the shaping of matter under the sway of ideal form – has taken a dystopian turn so that plasticity itself has become a destructive aesthetic vector. But it also reveals the toxicity of this ambiguity.

Figure C.1 Diana Lelonek, *Centre for Living Things*, 2016–. Courtesy of the artist.

Such toxicity, as Mel Y. Chen argues, can nevertheless be seized upon to consider the fundamental queerness of bodies and social forms.[2] Thus, in the age of plastic, while the condition of biological life has been so endangered by the plastic industry, its toxicity might nevertheless be the ground on which to reconsider the existential, ethical and aesthetic terms of normative relations. Plastic's toxicity has therefore become a fundamental materialist challenge by which to anticipate future social, cultural and environmental forms.

Notes

1 Jason Moore, 'The Capitalocene Part I: On the nature and origins of our ecological crisis', *The Journal of Peasant Studies* 44:3 (2017), 595.
2 Mel Y. Chen, 'Toxic animacies, inanimate affections', *GLQ: A Journal of Lesbian and Gay Studies* 17:2–3 (2011), pp. 265–86.

Data waste: the environmental and democratic problems associated with data-driven infrastructures

Roxana Vatanparast and Elettra Bietti

Figure D.0 Nina Mathijsen, *Collage D*, 2021. © takeadetour.eu. Courtesy of the artist.

Network and platform data-intensive technologies afford specific environmental risks. Amazon, for example, has announced intentions to be carbon-neutral by 2040, yet its platform operations contribute to significant carbon emissions.[1] Amazon also contributes to environmental harms in indirect ways through its provision of cloud-computing services to the oil and gas industry,[2] and its donations to political candidates denying climate change.[3]

Amazon's practices are just one example of the environmental impacts of data-driven technologies. They also reflect a broader phenomenon related to data-intensive commercial practices today. Empirical findings have shown that digital technologies contribute to 4 per cent of overall greenhouse gas emissions, a number expected to double by 2025.[4] Other estimates indicate that training a single artificial intelligence (AI) model emits carbon dioxide in amounts comparable to that of five cars over their lifetimes,[5] and that bitcoin mining consumes more electricity than the country of Switzerland.[6]

While much legal scholarship relating to data collection and processing has focused on individual privacy and autonomy, far less attention has been paid to the environmental impacts of data. In this contribution, we highlight a phenomenon we call 'data waste',[7] or the carbon emissions, natural resource extraction, production of waste and other harmful environmental impacts directly or indirectly attributable to data-driven infrastructures. These include platform-based business models (e.g. Amazon, Google), the programming and use of AI systems (e.g. machine learning and large language models such as OpenAI's GPT-3 and Google's BERT), and blockchain-based technologies (e.g. cryptocurrencies such as Bitcoin that are built on a permissionless distributed ledger technology that use proof of work consensus mechanisms).

We first describe data-driven infrastructures as reflecting an ideology of permissionless innovation and as producing network effects that tend toward monopolisation. We then explain how these factors have shaped data-driven infrastructures' impact on the climate. Next, we discuss how law and legal institutions have facilitated these developments and call for a more systemic understanding of the factors contributing to data waste. We end with a call to frame the issue of data waste as a sociotechnical controversy that raises broader questions about the power dynamics that underlie data-driven infrastructures and the need to imagine alternatives.

Data-driven infrastructures

Data-driven infrastructures are here defined widely as technologies that are fuelled by data and that generate data. Data, in other words, is both an input and an output of these technologies, in that it is both produced by such infrastructures, and what allows them to function. Examples of data-driven infrastructures include content-sharing platforms such as Facebook, YouTube, Twitter, Google and Amazon; AI systems that rely on data for their training and functioning and also produce new data, relying on the idea that 'bigger is better';[8] and blockchain-based systems, which rely on and produce information in the form of ledgers. Data-driven infrastructures also depend on material infrastructures for storing, transporting and processing data, such as data centres and data servers, which depend on intensive energy[9] and water[10] usage. Data-driven infrastructures therefore exist at multiple infrastructural layers.[11]

Data-intensive infrastructures have two specificities that distinguish them from other technologies. The first characteristic is their genealogical connection to logics of 'permissionless innovation' and 'generativity'. Permissionless innovation and generativity relate to a technology's capacity to let people innovate and build upon it without permission and in unforeseen ways. The second characteristic of data-intensive infrastructures is that they accelerate the monopolisation of digital markets. These infrastructures enable and incentivise business models based on connecting increasing numbers of people, capturing their attention and profiting from their data. Data-intensive infrastructures are often characterised by network effects; their functionality improves with the number of people using them and the amount of data collected through them, driving a vicious cycle of data extraction. The success of these business models depends on winner-takes-all monopolisation, achieved through network dynamics and strategies aimed at excluding rivals.

The way the internet was initially structured, as a layered end-to-end network, enabled innovation to take place at the user-interface level without interference from those who control the physical backbones of the internet. This led to a vision of the internet as an open ecosystem that enabled permissionless innovation – a space where anyone could develop disruptive projects without top-down checks or restraints. A similar principle applies to permissionless blockchain technologies which rely on an open distributed ledger. Behind their appearance as frictionless infrastructures, however, these technologies hide a darker side. They channel and amplify a culture of unreflective innovation which, if left unchecked, can lead to negative externalities – including data waste – while responsibility for those harms remains diffuse.

The combination of permissionless innovation and network effects that concentrate market power is driving ever-increasing data processing and storage, content and particularly video streaming in real time, and complex data analytics systems – all of which require intensive energy usage.[12] For example, to compete and generate revenues, tech giants such as Google and Facebook (Meta) fuel an aggressive culture of constant virtual connection for all, a culture largely powered through video content made salient by the success of platforms such as YouTube, Instagram or Twitch, one that may also be advancing in the Global South through cheap mobile devices and phone contracts.[13] The constant connection inherent in these business models comes with a substantial increase in data collection and waste.

In addition to contributing high amounts of global carbon emissions every year, global tech companies collaborate with oil companies, fund anti-climate change political campaigns and have detrimental effects on the climate in numerous other invisible ways. Network effects and concentrated market power are tied to environmental harms, as well as the power to shape public debates on climate change through political donations. Thus, data-driven infrastructures, market power and the political discourse around environmental issues cannot be disentangled from data waste.

The role of law

The early history of permissionless innovation is linked to the ideology of 'lawlessness', or the idea that innovation flourishes in the absence of regulatory constraints and that there exists an independent lawless space called cyberspace.[14] Indeed, in the USA, for instance, the dominant discourse in the tech industry is that self-regulation and self-governance promote innovation. This might be attributable to the assumption that law perpetually lags behind innovation, and therefore law should take a reactive role and defer to the authority of technologists in order not to hinder innovation.[15]

This idea, of course, reflects a limited view of the interaction between law, technology and society. Cyberspace and data-driven infrastructures are and have always been far from lawless. Lawyers use private law mechanisms to code assets into capital.[16] Tech companies, as owners of data-driven infrastructures, use these mechanisms to create and protect the wealth they obtain through data markets.[17] At the same time, legal rights, privileges and immunities have assured the reproducibility of economic and political power through information technologies.[18] Changes in US antitrust doctrine, and the challenges brought by technology corporations that no longer fit within the 'consumer welfare' antitrust model based on short-term price effects, have also contributed to the concentration of market power of companies like Amazon.[19] Moreover, in the USA, campaign finance laws protect corporate financing of political candidates based on freedom of speech principles,[20] giving tech companies opportunities to shape public discourse and policy. At a more fundamental level, law affects the relative bargaining power between technology corporations and users,[21] which facilitates tech corporations' endless accumulation of data from users and determines how gains from the data economy are distributed. Finally, international environmental law's role in managing global waste and the externalisation of waste by market mechanisms shapes the global distributive effects of data waste.[22] To say that data-driven infrastructures are self-regulated or that data waste is a result of lawlessness would therefore overlook a wide variety of legal mechanisms and institutions that have contributed to the phenomenon, and the broader legal arrangements which form part of the social fabric which technology embeds and in which it is embedded.[23]

Conclusion

The concerns raised here are not how to rein in the harmful environmental effects of data processing by creating more so-called 'sustainable tech' or 'green tech',[24] or by creating newer and better legal and policy frameworks around these particular environmental harms. Rather, the data waste generated through the operation of data-intensive infrastructures raises a sociotechnical controversy. Calls for technical fixes, such as moving to greener technologies to address climate change, reflect the same visions of social progress that contributed to where we are now. Technology cannot fix social and political problems alone. What is needed instead is political engagement on these issues and a systemic understanding of how data-intensive infrastructures, the social and legal constructs that contribute to their expansion, and the people building and designing them are collectively causing environmental harm and shaping futures for humanity and the planet. Data waste,

Figure D.1 Tom Ravenscroft, *TeleHouse North 2 at East India Dock campus*, 2016. Courtesy of the architect.

at its core, is a democratic and distributional problem. It requires engagement not only from engineers, experts and policymakers, but also democratic publics.

Notes

1. Amazon Sustainability – US, 'Our carbon footprint', <https://sustainability.aboutamazon.com/environment/carbon-footprint> [accessed 26 October 2022].
2. Brian Merchant, 'Amazon is aggressively pursuing big oil as it stalls out on clean energy', *Gizmodo*, 8 April 2019 <https://gizmodo.com/amazon-is-aggressively-pursuing-big-oil-as-it-stalls-ou-1833875828> [accessed 26 October 2022].
3. David McCabe & Karen Weise, 'Bezos and Zuckerberg take their pitches to Washington', *New York Times*, 19 September 2019 <https://www.nytimes.com/2019/09/19/business/bezos-zuckerberg-washington.html>.
4. Maxime Efoui-Hess, 'Climate crisis: The unsustainable use of online video', The Shift Project, 11 July 2019 <https://theshiftproject.org/wp-content/uploads/2019/07/2019-02.pdf> [accessed 26 October 2022].
5. Karen Hao, 'Training a single AI model can emit as much carbon as five cars in their lifetimes', *MIT Technology Review*, 6 June 2019 <https://www.technologyreview.com/s/613630/training-a-single-ai-model-can-emit-as-much-carbon-as-five-cars-in-their-lifetimes/>; Emma Strubell, Ananya Ganesh & Andrew McCallum, 'Energy and policy considerations for deep learning in NLP', in *Proceedings of the 57th Annual Meeting of the Association for Computational Linguistics* (Florence, Italy, 2019) pp. 3645–50, <http://arxiv.org/abs/1906.02243> [accessed 30 December 2022].
6. James Vincent, 'Bitcoin consumes more energy than Switzerland, according to new estimate', *The Verge*, 4 July 2019 <https://www.theverge.com/2019/7/4/20682109/bitcoin-energy-consumption-annual-calculation-cambridge-index-cbeci-country-comparison> [accessed 26 October 2022].

7 On the wastefulness of data generated on a daily basis, see Ron Bianchini, 'Are data centers the new global landfill?', *Wired*, October 2012 <https://www.wired.com/insights/2012/10/data-centers-new-global-landfill/> [accessed 26 October 2022]. Others have referred to the generation of data as a 'digital pollutant', a 'new kind of trash for the information age': Tyler Elliot Bettilyon, 'How data hoarding is the new threat to privacy and climate change', *Medium*, 1 August 2019 <https://onezero.medium.com/how-data-hoarding-is-the-new-threat-to-privacy-and-climate-change-1e5a21a49494> [accessed 26 October 2022]. Nanna Bonde Thylstrup frames 'digital traces' as a question of waste, which create social and environmental problems that 'follow gendered and colonial structures of violence': Nanna Bonde Thylstrup, 'Data out of place: toxic traces and the politics of recycling', *Big Data & Society* 6:2 (2019), pp. 1–2. Similarly, interdisciplinary workshops and research projects have been organised around addressing issues of waste in the context of big data. See e.g. 'Making waste, talking trash', *Digital Humanitarianism: Law & Policy Challenges* (UNSW Australia Faculty of Law, 2018) <https://datapolicy.law.unsw.edu.au/resources> [accessed 26 October 2022].

8 'Bigger is better' in this context refers to the belief that AI models that use mass computation are more accurate and thus 'better': Roel Dobbe & Meredith Whittaker, AI Now Institute, 'AI and climate change: How they're connected, and what we can do about it', *Medium*, 17 October 2019 <https://medium.com/@AINowInstitute/ai-and-climate-change-how-theyre-connected-and-what-we-can-do-about-it-6aa8d0f5b32c> [accessed 26 October 2022].

9 Sean Cubitt, *Finite Media: Environmental implications of digital technologies* (Duke University Press, 2017), pp. 16–21.

10 Mél Hogan, 'Data flows and water woes: The Utah Data Center', *Big Data & Society* 2:2 (2015), p. 1.

11 Yochai Benkler, 'From consumers to users: Shifting the deeper structures of regulation toward sustainable commons and user access', *Federal Communications Law Journal* 52 (1999), p. 561.

12 Cubitt, *Finite Media*.

13 Privacy International, 'Buying a smart phone on the cheap? Privacy might be the price you have to pay', 20 September 2019 <https://privacyinternational.org/long-read/3226/buying-smart-phone-cheap-privacy-might-be-price-you-have-pay> [accessed 26 October 2022].

14 John Perry Barlow, 'A declaration of the independence of cyberspace', *Duke Law & Technology Review* 18:1 (2019), pp. 5–7.

15 This idea refers to the 'law lag' narrative prevalent in dominant discourses on law's relationship to science and technology, which fails to take into account their interactive relationship in ordering society. See Sheila Jasanoff, 'Making order: Law and science in action', in *The Handbook of Science and Technology Studies*, ed. by Edward J. Hackett, Michael Lynch & Judy Wajcman (MIT Press, 2008), pp. 761–86.

16 Katharina Pistor, *The Code of Capital* (Princeton University Press, 2019).

17 Julie E. Cohen, *Between Truth and Power* (Oxford University Press, 2019).

18 Cohen, *Between Truth and Power*.

19 Lina Khan, 'Amazon's antitrust paradox', *Yale Law Journal* 126 (2017), pp. 710–805.

20 *Citizens United v. Federal Election Commission*, 558 U.S. 310 (2010), <https://www.supremecourt.gov/opinions/boundvolumes/558bv.pdf> [in the pdf, see p. 310 of the Reporter; accessed 30 December 2022].

21 Duncan Kennedy, 'The stakes of law, or Hale and Foucault', *Legal Studies Forum* 15 (1991), p. 327.

22 Olivier Barsalou & Michael Hennessy Picard, 'International environmental law in an era of globalized waste', *Chinese Journal of International Law* 17:3 (2018), pp. 887–906.

23 Jasanoff, 'Making order'; *States of Knowledge*, ed. by Sheila Jasanoff (Taylor & Francis, 2004).

24 Roy Schwartz et al., 'Green AI', *Communications of the ACM* 63:12 (2020), pp. 54–63.

Excrement

Franziska Neumann

Figure E.0 Nina Mathijsen, *Collage E*, 2021. © takeadetour.eu. Courtesy of the artist.

In 1758, Thomas Hale wrote in his *Compleat Body of Husbandry* that human excrement and urine were excellent fertilisers, though he then added, '[a]s to its use … there is something so distasteful, not to say shocking, in the thought'.[1] In short, human excrement remained a potent fertiliser, though consumers may have found the idea disgusting. In his view, London was an enormous and unused source of manure, given the sheer number of people who used the latrine every day. In fact, excrement was one of the key waste materials in the early modern city. Assuming, at a very conservative estimate, that the average adult in the early modern period produced at least 50 grams of faeces per day, this meant about 37.5 tons of faecal matter produced daily across the whole of mid-eighteenth-century London. The matter had to be disposed of somewhere. Consequently, sewage as a waste material became an integral part of urban metabolic cycles: beginning mostly in residential latrines, then transported in the barrows of the latrine cleaners known as nightmen, and eventually used in the fields of nearby farms as manure.

The example of Thomas Hale shows that excrement as a waste material is a social challenge as much as a material one. Excrement is intimately linked to notions of uncleanness, danger and disorder, or, as Samuel Johnson put it in 1755 in *A Dictionary of the English Language*: '*Excrement*. That which is thrown out as useless, noxious, or corrupted from the natural passages of the body.'[2]

In the eighteenth century, excrement and the locus of human waste were not necessarily considered repulsive. They could also be a matter of curiosity or economic interest. Scatological texts were in vogue, with titles ranging from *A Meditation on T[ur]d, Wrote in a Place of Ease* (1727) to the extremely popular *The Benefit of Farting Explained* (1722). Through the medium of excrement, it was possible to negotiate the human condition; those who spoke about excrement also implicitly and explicitly spoke about urbanity, the public and the private sphere, and the relationship between body, decency and gender. Isaac Cruikshank's 1799 print *Indecency* (Figure E.1) is particularly revealing, depicting a scantily clad woman relieving herself on the street. The visual language leaves no doubt as to what kind of woman she is: Broad Street was notorious for street prostitution. Instead of the domestic sphere, the prostitute uses the public space; rather than being coy, she addresses the viewer directly: 'What are you staring at?' Caricatures like these play with taboos by showing female urination in public or semi-public spaces, countering any notion of female decency.

As waste matter, excrement was an everyday experience for city dwellers, albeit an unpleasant one. Yet hardly any other waste material shows one fact so clearly: waste is not just a material that has to be disposed of. Excrement is highly symbolic. How we deal with it offers insights – sometimes delightful, sometimes disgusting – into the social imaginary of societies.

Figure E.1 Isaac Cruikshank, *Indecency*, 1799. London: S.W. Fores. Photograph. © Library of Congress Prints and Photographs Division.

Notes

1 Thomas Hale, *A Compleat Body of Husbandry* […], Vol. I, 2nd ed. (London, 1758), p. 158.
2 Samuel Johnson, *A Dictionary of the English Language* […], vol. I (London, 1755), o.p.

Fire: burning down the house of memory

Stamatis Zografos

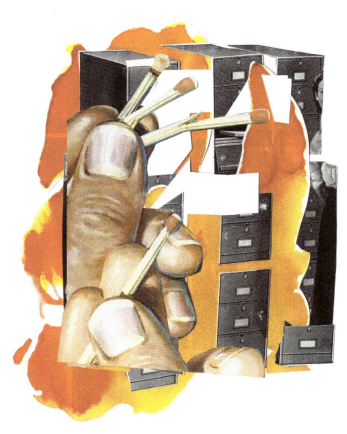

Figure F.0 Nina Mathijsen, *Collage F*, 2021. © takeadetour.eu. Courtesy of the artist.

A widespread pathology of contemporary culture is its hysterical, nearly fetishised relationship to memory. Andreas Huyssen detected early symptoms towards the end of the twentieth century, which he refers to as the 'twilight of memory' due to its exhaustive obsession with memory's preservation.[1] Over two decades since this diagnosis, our condition has significantly deteriorated, for today memory never goes to waste. Intentionally or not, we preserve every aspect of our contemporary life and culture, forming a huge, gradually expanding archive of countless memories that threatens to acquire the status of an Aleph, the point in space that Jorge Louis Borges once witnessed, which contains the entire knowledge of the 'inconceivable universe'.[2] In *Architecture and Fire*, I argue that buildings operate as archives, for they absorb and preserve memory.[3] The association of buildings with the function of the archive allows for a reading of architecture through the archival theory elaborated by Jacques Derrida. According to Derrida, archives are characterised by violence (*Gewalt*), an innate power 'which at once posits and conserves the law'.[4] Archives, including buildings, are therefore places where power is exercised, and memory imposed.

Derrida's theory, developed out of a creative encounter with psychoanalysis, further suggests that archives carry with them intrinsically an opposing impulse, namely 'archive fever': the desire to return to the origin, to the primordial memory. This he likens to the Freudian death drive, the tendency that pushes both towards an inorganic state and towards the destruction of memory.[5] Seen in this light, the physical destruction of memory-sites testifies to our obsessive attachment to memory and prescribes a course of action that could contribute to our collective physical and mental wellbeing. I suggest that recent outbreaks of fire in scenes of urban unrest can therefore be read as violent expressions of the modern archival condition. Hong Kongers recently set fires throughout their city, protesting against leader Carrie Lam's policies; parts of London and other cities in the United Kingdom were severely burnt during the riots in 2011; protesters lit fires in cities in Egypt, Syria, Libya and Tunisia during the Arab Spring; Athens has repeatedly been devastated by fire during protests against austerity. What stands out from these scenes of violence is the intense imagery of flames consuming lives, hopes, buildings and the urban landscape. The last memory of these scenes of violence is what fire leaves behind, its ashes. An archival reading accepts this urban violence as an innate expression of the archive as embodied in the building, and fire as the externalisation of the death drive.

Let us return to my initial proposition: that contemporary culture's obsessive preservation of memory leads to an over-accumulation of

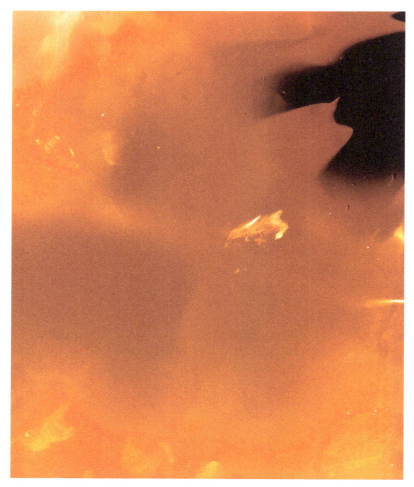

Figure F.1   Rhona Eve Clews, *Coax*, 2018. Courtesy of the artist.

memory, which in turn incubates an ever-expanding archive. In line with Derrida's psychoanalytic reading of the archive, this behaviour portends the archive's violent eruptions. Hence my proposal, now, that part of the archive's content must necessarily go to waste – although not necessarily in catastrophic outbreaks of fire. If we are to avoid these violent expressions of archive fever, we must learn how to externalise our death drive and let things go in other ways.

Notes

1 Andreas Huyssen, *Twilight Memories: Marking time in a culture of amnesia* (Routledge, 1995), p. 3.
2 Jorge Luis Borges, *The Aleph: Including the prose fictions from The Maker* (Penguin, 2000), p. 131.
3 Stamatis Zografos, *Architecture and Fire: A psychoanalytic approach to conservation* (UCL Press, 2019), p. 170.
4 Jacques Derrida, *Archive Fever*, translated by Eric Prenowitz (University of Chicago Press, 1995), p. 7.
5 Derrida, *Archive Fever*, p. 91.

Ground up

Onya McCausland

Figure G.0 Nina Mathijsen, *Collage G*, 2021. © takeadetour.eu. Courtesy of the artist.

The Coal Authority manages over 82 mine-water treatment schemes across Britain, handling and treating over 122 billion litres of mine water every year. The schemes prevent up to 4,000 tonnes of iron solids from entering and polluting local watercourses. If the water is left untreated, the ferric oxyhydroxide residues (or 'ochre') pollute and stain riverbeds, turning them orange.

Scattered across the UK, these mine-water treatment schemes take the form of brightly coloured orange lakes marking the ground where coal and metal mine infrastructure used to be. The pumps that once kept the mines dry, so that they could be worked, have been switched back on to prevent mine-water levels from contaminating drinking or ground water. Each scheme contains three to four settling 'lagoons' where the iron-rich mine water is pumped to the surface, forming newly oxidised minerals; iron solids accumulate by sedimenting to the bottom of the lakes, while the water, now separated from the ochre, is syphoned off and diverted back into the rivers. Every few years the lagoons are emptied of their thick orange sediment, so they can begin to fill again. This process goes on and on; minerals will wash through the mines continually for decades, even hundreds of years to come.

Dealing with one problem causes another. This leaky mopping-up operation is a continual visible reminder of how parts of the land were once used. And despite every effort to keep the sites and their former function hidden from view, they remain highly visible. Each site is

Figure G.1 Six Bells Mine Water Treatment Scheme 51°43 33.56 N 3°07 58.63 W 638 m. ©2019 Google.

individual, idiosyncratic, its pragmatic design informed by the lie of the land, its location determined by the invisible carved architecture beneath the surface.

The material junk of the mining industry gurgles back up to the surface, betraying all those hidden holes in the ground. The orange ochre sludge forming here forever is now part of the scene of the British landscape. Paradoxically, this material that now forms as waste, and is periodically sent to landfill, once represented a more symbiotic relationship between humans and the earth: a material so revered, with roots in the beginnings of human cultural activity, that it was used in life-giving ritual performance. Red ochre was a symbol of fertility and strength; the blood of the earth was so important that it was thought to carry humans safely through the underworld to their next life; iron, ochre, haematite, synonymous with red blood, reversed the transition from life to death.

It turns out that, if ground up into a fine powder, the material pouring out of the mines can be used as a pigment – a colour that contains the history of a different relationship between humans and the earth.

Hairs

Robyn Adams

Figure H.0 Nina Mathijsen, *Collage H*, 2021. © takeadetour.eu. Courtesy of the artist.

The cultural history of reading is a tale of the fervent relationships between readers and their books. We might think of reading as a largely cerebral act, of words and thoughts sinuously flowing between page and brain. Yet books are physical objects, and the traces of reading encounters often remain. On the exterior, shabby bindings and tattered page edges testify to the dynamic use experienced by many volumes. The interior possesses numerous areas which present a suitable canvas to trap the sediment of reading: within the central gutter of the pages can lurk microscopic detritus accumulated over centuries, such as dust, soot, pollen, sand, fibres, food and chemical powders. Very often, the book historian discovers hairs trapped in the interstices of the book, a legacy perhaps of the ardent connection of the reader to the book coupled with the happy deficiency of the conservator's cleaning brush or vacuum. These can present as single strands, tufts or eyelashes. Presumably, most hairs are human, but perhaps some are canine, feline or rodent, suggesting alternate users of the book and its proximal environs.

What is left behind, then, when a reader finishes reading? Can the shedding of hair also shed light on historic reading practices and habits? Human hairs materially entangled with the book offer more than signals of use, ownership and hirsuteness of reader. The material turn in textual history has witnessed hair and other waste particles being analysed for evidence of readers' gender, disease and geographical origin. What some might see as banal waste, others see as archaeological evidence for the history of reading, analysis of which viscerally confirms the provenance of the textual item. DNA analysis on dust bunnies caught in the folds

Figure H.1   Pareid Architecture, *Follicle*, 2019. Courtesy of the architects.

of sixteenth-century books has confirmed the presence of microbial DNA (skin bacteria and fungi). The book as a substrate for waste and bodily deposits does not attract only scientists and scholars: an artist has recently cultured bacteria from her own blood wiped over pages of eighteenth-century poetry.

In this way we must go in between and beyond the pages and text block of the book, to peer into the dusty corners of paper, leather and ink and to ask, what were the conditions in which the hair and other matter fell into the book? Were tired eyes rubbed to dislodge a lash? Did the construing of a difficult passage occasion the scratching of hair from the scalp? Why are some books hairier than others? If analysed and sequenced, these accidental hairy remains can potentially tell us as much about the reader – if not more – as the ownership inscriptions found on the frangible pages of rare volumes. This unwanted sediment offers a new frontier of evidence and examination, giving new valency to the waste generated by historic readers.

Identity

Caitlin DeSilvey

Figure I.0 Nina Mathijsen, *Collage I*, 2021. © takeadetour.eu. Courtesy of the artist.

What (and how) we waste says as much about who we are, and who we want to be, as what we consume. Over a decade ago, scholarship on waste and identity emerged to provide a counterpoint to research on consumption subjectivities, with geographers offering critical insights.[1] Their work described practices of discard, disinvestment and disposal as essential to the maintenance of a coherent and legible self. When I ask students on my Waste and Society module to reflect on what they left behind when they moved out of their family homes to attend university, they describe how the shedding of possessions was also a shedding of versions of themselves that they had outgrown. They also often mention the things they could not bring themselves to part with – the threadbare T-shirts and the old phones – because they held too many 'core memories'.[2] The relation between self and things is something we learn young. In a recent clear-out I discarded my four-year-old's collection of foam bath letters – the ethylene-vinyl acetate speckled with mould and chew marks. When he realised I had dispatched them to the rubbish bin, he wailed, 'But I love them!' 'Sometimes when things get old, they get worn out and you have to throw them away,' I explained. In anguish, he cried, 'Sometimes when things get old, they get precious!' Part of his small self was bound up with those letters, and he was reluctant to let that go.

This kind of thinking assumes that the self is a relatively bounded thing that can be maintained as a coherent entity through intentional behaviour, including periodic thinning of our possessions. This conception of the self also underpins research on how 'waste behaviours' align with values, as people express their identities through diligent recycling, or by adopting zero-waste lifestyles.[3] Acts of wasting (or not wasting) are linked to the maintenance of specific subjectivities, and moralities. But, as Greg Kennedy points out, waste can also work to trouble these conceptions of the self as singular and stable.[4] Drawing on both Heidegger and the teachings of Buddhism, he explores how contemplation of the disposable can prompt us to acknowledge the inter-penetration between ourselves and a wider world of beings, in a 'network of mutual relations'.[5] The self, in such a framing, becomes a porous and relational entity, rather than the preserve of a bounded and coherent subject.

A quick scan of the news headlines presents alarming evidence of interpenetration and porosity, as the chemical and material legacy of our possessions, and everyday practices, comes back to haunt us: 'Clothes washing linked to "pervasive" plastic pollution in the Arctic'; '"Forever chemicals" pollute water from Alaska to Florida';

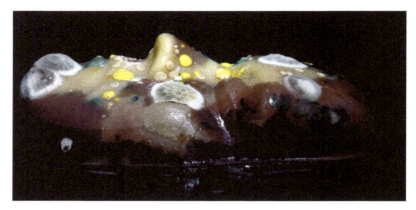

Figure I.1 Mellissa Fisher, *Microbial Me*, 2015. In collaboration with Professor Mark Clements and Dr Richard Harvey. Supported by ThermoFisher Scientific. Courtesy of the artist.

'Human activity to push CO2 concentration in the atmosphere over 50 per cent above pre-industrial levels in 2021'; 'Microplastics found in human placentas'. If the relation between waste and identity was once conceived of as an extension of housekeeping (to self-keeping), it is increasingly complicated by the awareness that the things we thought we had discarded (or, worse, that we didn't think about at all) are still with us: in our cells, in our food, in our water and in the living systems we share the world with. We are defined by what and how we waste, yes; but rather than placing this waste on the other side of a safe boundary, we now are forced to recognise that the boundary was always a fiction. 'A permanently polluted world is one that, because of its deep alteration, reclaims the need to incite new forms of response-ability'[6] – and this will require new forms of subjectivity. Beyond the bounded self, we may come to understand self as sponge – contaminated, complicit and contingent (like those mouldy foam letters) – but perhaps providing an opening to more care-ful ways of being in the world.

Notes

1 Nicky Gregson, Alan Metcalfe & Louise Crewe, 'Identity, mobility, and the throwaway society', *Environment and Planning D: Society and Space* 25 (2007), pp. 682–700; Kevin Hetherington, 'Secondhandedness: Consumption, disposal, and absent presence', *Environment and Planning D: Society and Space* 22 (2004), pp. 157–73; Louise Crewe, 'Life itemised: Lists, loss, unexpected significance, and the enduring geographies of discard', *Environment and Planning D: Society and Space* 29 (2011), pp. 27–46.

2   Deborah L. Cabaniss, 'Inside "Inside Out"', *The Lancet Psychiatry* 2 (2015), p. 789.
3   Stewart Barr et al., 'Beyond recycling: An integrated approach for understanding municipal waste management', *Applied Geography* 39 (2013), pp. 67–77; Natália Pietzsch et al., 'Benefits, challenges and critical factors of success for Zero Waste: A systematic literature review', *Waste Management* 67 (2017), pp. 324–53.
4   Greg Kennedy, *An Ontology of Trash: The disposable and its problematic nature* (SUNY Press, 2007).
5   Kennedy, *An Ontology of Trash*, p. 35.
6   Max Liboiron, Manuel Tironi & Nerea Calvillo, 'Toxic politics: Acting in a permanently polluted world', *Social Studies of Science* 48 (2018), pp. 331–49, p. 332.

Junk bonds

David Sim

Figure J.0 Nina Mathijsen, *Collage J*, 2021. © takeadetour.eu. Courtesy of the artist.

Figure J.1 Hilary Powell and the Bank Job team, *Big Bang 2: Debt explosion*, 2019. Photograph by Graeme Truby.

Junk bonds promise great reward and the obvious chance of default. They were ubiquitous across the nineteenth-century United States of America, which was home to a market in distant revolutions. If you wanted to buy into insurrection elsewhere – in Ireland, say, or in Cuba – you were welcome to play the odds, buying the bonds issued by nationalist organisations. Doing so – investing in a revolution happening outside the USA – required a leap of faith to imagine a geopolitical state of affairs that was at odds, sometimes radically so, with immediate reality. Some of these opportunities were probably shakedowns. Some were legitimate. Some of those would-be nation-states who issued bonds came into being and paid out. Others did not. All were junk, until they weren't.

Bonds had financial significance, of course. They were printed IOUs, approximating banknotes, backed by whatever revolutionaries could promise potential buyers. They also had social, emotional and political weight. Nationalists, secessionists and anti-imperialists could superficially embrace the cold logic of the bond market even as they made a claim for legitimacy on behalf of a specifically defined group claiming self-determination. Participating in this market was a way for Americans, whether native-born or immigrant, to demonstrate their solidarity with such movements elsewhere. These bonds also served as a form of social glue, binding together diasporic constituencies who committed their limited savings to supporting insurrection and liberation back home. In addition, they helped build diasporic connections between citizen and nation, even where that nation-state remained speculative.

We often think about this in ideological or affective terms: a commitment to liberalism, say, or to national self-determination. And we think in terms of statesmen, and speeches, and texts. But small-bill investments in bonds, sold in minor denominations in the immigrant neighbourhoods of American cities – the debt of countries that did not exist and might never exist – give us a window into a world of transnational community and revolutionary sympathy in this period. The people purchasing these bonds might never have seen the place they were investing in. If they had, they might never see it again. But these bonds allowed people with little capital to participate in a form of everyday diasporic transnationalism, as individuals who could engage in transnational community-building in their immediate locales. You might not get your money back, and you might not secure those great rewards. They might, ultimately, prove worthless. But they were hardly junk.

Kinship (chemical)

Angeliki Balayannis

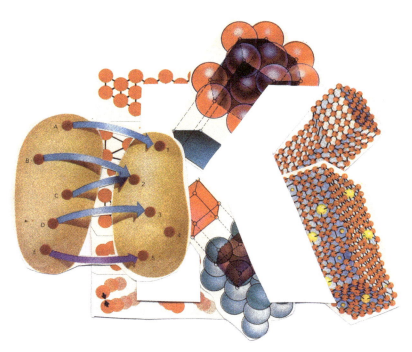

Figure K.0 Nina Mathijsen, *Collage K*, 2021. © takeadetour.eu. Courtesy of the artist.

In 2012, a 220-tonne chemical stockpile was incinerated in the Veolia hazardous waste disposal facility in Dąbrowa Górnicza, Poland. This incinerator is designed to destroy wastes deemed too politically and materially hazardous for landfill or recycling – materials too unruly for the closed loops of the circular economy. A cloud steadily billows from its steel smokestack: an uncertain mixture of vapours, gases and particulate matter. The toxic capacities of incinerator emissions are a matter of concern for environmental activists. However, the material politics of this process extends far beyond fence line communities. To fully attend to the ethics of incineration, it is necessary to follow the wastes which feed these facilities.

Before arriving at Dąbrowa Górnicza, the chemical stockpile – largely constituted of banned and expired formulations of DDT – had been slowly deteriorating in a concrete storage shed in the village of Vikuge, in eastern Tanzania. It was dumped in Vikuge in 1986, although the origins of these chemicals remain uncertain. This is one example of the 'toxic waste colonialism'[1] which emerged in the wake of Rachel Carson's *Silent Spring* (1962), as a generation of synthetic chemicals were becoming banned and restricted. The pesticides were (visibly) removed from their storage site to be incinerated as part of a continent-wide World Bank pesticide disposal programme. But these persistent organic pollutants continue to linger and accumulate in many of the bodies they have encountered in Vikuge village, and far beyond.[2]

The removal of this stockpile rendered this situation politically invisible.[3] Figure K.1 is a photograph of the pesticides which faced the furnace in Dąbrowa Górnicza. The bottles mark their manufacturers, indicating that they were made for distribution in Greece. The incineration process transformed this stockpile in molecular terms

Figure K.1 Angeliki Balayannis, *SARPI-Veolia incinerator smoke stack*, Dąbrowa Górnicza, Poland, 2016. Courtesy of the author.

but also destroyed labels, bottles and distinctive chemical signatures. This information is necessary to commodify, govern, manage and make sense of chemicals and their effects. Industrial chemicals are 'informed materials':[4] assemblages of matter and information. The combustion of this stockpile was also the destruction of evidence.

All that remained from the incineration process were rumours and grainy snapshots archived by concerned chemists who have studied the stockpile's residues. Destroying these informed materials has made justice difficult for affected communities in Tanzania and research challenging for environmental chemists.[5] Like other World Bank development interventions, it works to compound the original violence by creating erasures.[6] The material and administrative destructiveness of incineration generates questions around how to approach the toxic legacies of twentieth-century chemistry more carefully.

To avoid severing relations of responsibility and accountability, geographers are calling for environmental interventions to approach technological monsters with care, collaboration and humility.[7] One way of enabling this is by imagining chemicals not as contaminants, but as kin. This is a messy more-than-human form of kinship that resists genealogical and reproductive modes of relating.[8] Learning from Vanessa Agard-Jones's work with chlordecone, feminist technoscience scholars have been developing 'chemical kinship' as a concept and practice for expanding spatial and temporal obligations to materials routinely reduced to their violence.[9] Chemical kinship can cultivate the publics assembling around shared exposures (along with their harms) and it decentres moralising discourses of 'bad' chemicals that need to be 'cleaned up'.

The material geographies of this chemical stockpile suggest that incineration can amplify the very injustices that environmental interventions seek to redress. This is not necessarily an argument against incineration, but a call to recognise that the destruction of toxic legacies is impossible. Responsibility for environmental violence requires *caring for* hazardous materials: a negative becoming that fosters (an uneasy) kinship with chemicals, to remember toxic legacies when practising detoxified futures.

Notes

1   Laura A. Pratt, 'Decreasing dirty dumping? A re-evaluation of toxic waste colonialism and the global management of transboundary hazardous waste', *William & Mary Environmental Law and Policy Review* 35 (2011), 582–623.

2 John Andrew Marco Mahugija, Bernhard Henkelmann & Karl-Werner Schramm, 'Levels and patterns of organochlorine pesticides and their degradation products in rainwater in Kibaha Coast Region, Tanzania', *Chemosphere* 118 (2015), pp. 12–19.
3 Angeliki Balayannis, 'Toxic sights: The spectacle of hazardous waste removal', *Environment and Planning D: Society & Space* 38 (2020), pp. 772–90.
4 Andrew Barry, 'Pharmaceutical matters: The invention of informed materials', *Theory, Culture & Society* 22 (2005), pp. 51–69.
5 Angeliki Balayannis, 'Routine exposures: Reimaging the visual politics of hazardous sites', *GeoHumanities* 5 (2019), pp. 572–90.
6 David Naguib Pellow, *Resisting Global Toxics: transnational movements for environmental justice* (MIT Press, 2007).
7 Caitlynn Beckett, 'Beyond remediation: Containing, confronting and caring for the Giant Mine Monster', *Environment and Planning E: Nature and Space* 4:4 (2021), pp. 1389–412.
8 Donna Haraway, *Staying with the Trouble: Making kin in the Chthulucene* (Duke University Press, 2016).
9 Vanessa Agard-Jones, 'Bodies in the system', *Small Axe* 17 (2013), pp. 182–92; Angeliki Balayannis & Emma Garnett, 'Chemical kinship: Interdisciplinary experiments with pollution', *Catalyst: Feminism, Theory, Technoscience* 6 (2020), pp. 1–10.

Land waste: an imaginary beast?

Sonia Freire Trigo

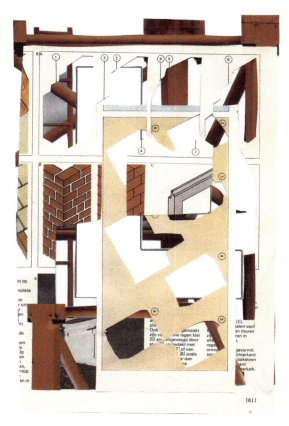

Figure L.0 Nina Mathijsen, *Collage L*, 2021. © takeadetour.eu. Courtesy of the artist.

Figure L.1   Hilary Powell, *The Games*, 2017. Courtesy of the artist.

Land waste can be understood as the biggest form of waste in our cities. It is commonly agreed that its presence poses a threat to the fundamental principle of efficient land use that underpins urban planning and development. Policymakers in central government have tried, time after time, to locate and measure land in England that is being 'wasted' – that is, not used to its full potential.[1] Yet tracking down this urban species can prove challenging, as land surveys have shown since the mid-1950s. Older and larger waste-lands, for example, usually camouflage themselves with ageing factories, imposing cranes and windswept landscapes. The smaller and younger waste-lands, on the other hand, tend to pop up around town centres, disguised as small warehouses or type B office space. Car parks and brutalist housing estates are other examples of the many forms these chameleonic creatures adopt in our built environments. Different concepts have tried to pin down over the years the diverse physical appearance of waste-land: derelict land; vacant land; previously developed land; brownfield land. Yet, the nature and extent of waste-land remains unclear … unless one wears the right pair of glasses.

When looking at land merely as a support for economic growth, waste-land pops up everywhere, especially in high-demand urban areas.[2] With those spectacles on, any piece of land that could hold a more valuable use appears as an ugly waste in urgent need of redevelopment. But a change of glasses reveals that not all 'underused land' is a waste. Some of it provides the necessary space for those low-valued economic activities that are essential for the normal functioning of our cities.[3] Some other such land has the capacity to bring back nature to the built environment.[4] In other cases, underused land offers an outdoor opportunity for communities to socialise and strengthen their agency in place-making processes.[5] Waste-lands are therefore imaginary beasts

Figure L.2 Sonia Freire Trigo, *Activities on 'vacant' land in the Vauxhall Nine Elms Battersea Opportunity Area, London*, 2012. Courtesy of the author.

Figure L.3 Sonia Freire Trigo, *Leftovers of the temporary uses of vacant land in the Royal Docks, London*, 2015. Courtesy of the author.

Figure L.4 Sonia Freire Trigo, *Time suspended over the vacant land on Silvertown Quays, London*, 2015. Courtesy of the author.

that mirror the values that society projects onto land. These beasts will keep roaming our built environments for as long as we look at land as a mere support for economic growth. If you are scared of waste-lands, just change your glasses.

Notes

1. David Adams, Christopher De Sousa & Steven Tiesdell, 'Brownfield development: A comparison of North American and British approaches', *Urban Studies*, 47 (2010), pp. 75–104; Sonia Freire Trigo, *Vacant Land in London: Narratives of people, space, and time* (unpublished doctoral thesis, UCL, 2019).
2. Sonia Freire Trigo, 'Vacant land in London: A planning tool to create land for growth', *International Planning Studies* 25 (2020), 261–76.
3. See, for example, Jessica Ferm & Edward Jones, 'Beyond the post-industrial city: Valuing and planning for industry in London', *Urban Studies* 54 (2017), pp. 3380–98.
4. Nélida R. Villaseñor et al., 'Vacant lands as refuges for native birds: An opportunity for biodiversity conservation in cities', *Urban Forestry & Urban Greening* 49 (2020), 126632.
5. David Jeevendrampillai, 'The making of a suburb', in *London's Urban Landscape: Another way of telling*, ed. by Christopher Tilley (UCL Press, 2019), pp. 178–203; Krystallia Kamvasinou, 'Temporary intervention and long-term legacy: Lessons from London case studies', *Journal of Urban Design* 22 (2017), 187–207.

Microbes

Elaine Cloutman-Green

Figure M.0 Nina Mathijsen, *Collage M*, 2021. © takeadetour.eu. Courtesy of the artist.

The word 'microbe' is a coverall term for parasites, viruses, bacteria and fungi. Although we often think about them as linked to human infection and of key importance in relation to medicine and health care, the agriculture and food production industry would be very different without them. Microbes are essential to processes such as fermentation, which provides bread and beer for our daily lives. One of the key areas of innovation and exploration moving forward is to better understand the natural properties of the microbes that surround us and how we can use both them and technologies to control them in order to address waste and energy issues linked to climate change.

Figure M.1   Sonja Bäumel, *Microbial entanglement*, Frankfurter Kunstverein, 2019. Photograph: copyright Robert Schittko.

2020 was the year of waste, especially for those of us working in health care. The environmental focus went out the window with the need for increased amounts of personal protective equipment to support safe practice during the COVID-19 pandemic. This means that, instead of reducing plastic, we've increased it by wearing more gloves, face masks and visors. Although the pandemic may have largely come to an end in some countries, its impact on health care and the increased use of protection are likely to continue for years, and for much longer in many parts of the world.

Within the Infection Prevention and Control team and the Estates team at Great Ormond Street Hospital, we've spent the last five years or so trying to reduce our impact on the environment. This has been done by introducing novel technologies to control infection risk, as well as evaluating items such as new decontamination techniques that reduce the amount of chemicals entering the water system. Hot-water systems within health care run at more than 60 degrees Celsius in order to control the growth of *Legionella pneumophila* bacteria, which can cause significant infections. By introducing the use of low-temperature water systems that control *Legionella* growth using silver copper ion dosing, it has been possible to reduce the need to heat water to 63 degrees Celsius, thus reducing environmental impact in carbon emissions by 22.31 tons of carbon dioxide per year in a single health centre – an amount of emissions equivalent to that produced by the electricity use of 3.8 British homes for a year.

Ironically, a problem caused by one type of microbe, the virus SARS-CoV-2 that causes COVID-19, may be addressed in part by another, a bacterium known as *Ideonella sakaiensis*. This bacterium and others like it can break down plastics (such as polyethylene terephthalate or PET, used to make water bottles) using an enzyme called PETase. Since its discovery, work is being undertaken to see if these enzymes and modified versions can be utilised more widely to process plastic waste faster than the naturally available microbe, even though this technology is not yet widely in use on a large scale.

Nalu

Melissa McCarthy

Figure N.0 Nina Mathijsen, *Collage N*, 2021. © takeadetour.eu. Courtesy of the artist.

Nalu is the Hawaiian word for 'wave'. Put it together with *he'e*, 'to slip or slide', and you have *he'e nalu* – 'surfing'. Waves aren't waste, though they result in froth or foam, extraneous matter, as the breaking wave releases the energy that's been gathering and travelling through the ocean.

But I'm thinking in the context of Miki Dora, a legendary figure from the period when surfing was emerging as an activity in the 1950s US West Coast. A professional contrarian, Dora built up his own mystique, to the extent that 'Dora lives' was a popular graffito seen after his absence from the Malibu scene, and various beach-related bon mots are attributed to him:

> Waves are the ultimate illusion.
> They come out of nowhere, instantaneously materialize, and just as quickly they break and vanish.
> Chasing after such fleeting mirages is a complete waste of time.
> That is what I choose to do with my life.

And

> If you are willing to accept the assertion that surfing is a colossal waste of time, then I'll concede I've wasted my life. But in a better and more graceful manner than any of my two-legged counterparts, no matter what the cost or consequences.

Pursuing the nalu; chasing the waves, choosing the waste, is Dora's self-justification. And perhaps any surfer's. After all, what happens? You paddle out to sea, you wait, you fall over, wipe out, fail to catch; or you make the ride in, and you're back exactly where you started.

Where else can we see an action of repetition, of failure, of moving without going anywhere: a strange and self-propelled stasis that is achieved by people treading the boards? In the plays of Samuel Beckett. *Endgame* (1958, first English publication) has on the austere stage two ashbins for Hamm's parents, with their wasted bodies.[1] 'Ashbins' is the word used in the stage directions; in other vernaculars they might be described as trashcans, dustbins, where Oscar lives in *Sesame Street*, metal receptacles. But in any language, containers for waste. And what happens in the play? Nothing, again and every day; only some desperate construction of the self through storytelling and language. There's a failure of language, of Hamm's 'babble, babble words' that he'll 'speak no more' – words dissipate like bubbles of ocean foam. But in this play, words are almost all that they've got. Hamm is explicit that 'it's story time', as he retells, refines, repeatedly performs to his captive audiences. It's the same self-mythologising that Dora, too, does, as he promulgates his own legend, as he insists on the value of surfing as the time-wasting done on the ocean wastes.

Beckett offers us waste as object, waste as blasted landscape – through the window, Clov sees 'Zero … zero … and zero' – and waste as verb. But he doesn't forget the nalu. 'The waves, how are the waves?' asks Hamm. Then he adds the vital question for anyone interested in surfing: 'Wait! Will there be sharks, do you think?'

Note

1 Samuel Beckett, *Endgame* (Faber, 1958).

Ñiquiñaque/extraÑo

Adriana Laura Massidda and Hanna Baumann

Figure Ñ.0 Nina Mathijsen, *Collage Ñ*, 2021. © takeadetour.eu. Courtesy of the artist.

ñiquiñaque: rare Spanish word meaning insignificant, 'despicable person or thing'.[1]

extraÑo: strange, unfamiliar; sometimes with a connotation of uncanniness.[2]

In his observational documentary *La multitud*,[3] Martín Oesterheld portrays a series of derelict spaces or 'urban interstices' in order to articulate a critical narrative about urban decay and transformation.[4] These include abandoned theme parks, car dumps and the edges of the 'Ecological Reserve'. A series of figures slide smoothly, almost speechless, across these spaces, linking two shantytowns, a social housing complex, a power plant and a set of top-end skyscrapers under construction.

The wastelands depicted reflect key junctions of Argentina's twentieth-century history. Built by the last dictatorship (Proceso de Reorganización Nacional, 1976–83) in accordance with a 1960s masterplan, the unprofitable amusement park Interama was left to rust. Echoing it, the Ciudad Deportiva de La Boca sports complex remains incomplete, its concrete ruins evocative of a moment of ambition and optimism coinciding with the presidency of Arturo Illia (1963–66) and the Revolución Argentina dictatorship (1966–73). Each park is bordered by the rusting remains of vehicles in official yet unregulated open-air car dumps. Vegetation is shown growing inside the cars and in the theme parks' imaginative concrete figures. Finally, swelling on the edge of the city, native and exotic plants of the Ecological Reserve grow on the rubble of the demolitions produced by the Proceso. In it, flora and fauna are protected by a municipal bylaw issued in the mid-1980s, in the context of cultural rejuvenation that marked Argentina's return to democracy. This blossoming of life contrasts with the memory of systematic kidnap, torture and murder that is evoked by the waste that supports it (the Proceso was, in fact, Argentina's most traumatic period of the century). This produces an unsettling effect reminiscent, *mutatis mutandis*, of the bombed-out *Brachen* (fallow lands) in divided post-war Berlin as described by Matthew Gandy, where political violence created the conditions that allowed new forms of urban nature to thrive.[5]

Urban margins, abandoned spaces and wastelands are often regarded as *ñiquiñaque*, as things to neglect and abhor. However, as Cristian Silva argues, interstices are, through their very marginality, key to fundamental urban processes such as sprawl, where they 'destabilize institutional orthodoxies'.[6] External to urban planning, they contribute to sprawl's fragmented nature. In the case of the interstices portrayed in *La multitud*, this disruptive quality is further highlighted by their proximity to more formalised spaces (the high-end constructions, the power plant, the housing complex), which makes them strangers, alien, *extraños* to their own context. I am here using the term *extraños* in line with Sigmund Freud's analysis of the *unheimlich*, 'something repressed which *recurs*',[7] something once familiar which was displaced to the unconscious and which re-emerges displaced, and which duplicates its appearances when it should have remained hidden, becoming profoundly distressing. This extends to the role of vegetation in the abandoned spaces observed: Oesterheld's portrayal of inhabited cars, a dried fountain hosting miniature trees and a mouldy giant Gulliver figure reminds us of the uncanniness produced by encountering life in unanimated objects, by the blurring of the boundary between the living and the dead,[8] and by the spanning of the artificial/natural divide which largely underpins our culture. By observing these spaces in their 'elegant deterioration',[9] Oesterheld brings to the fore the disturbing persistence of Argentina's recent past. Furthermore, in *La multitud*, marginal spaces once more become central: by focusing on two locations in the east and the southwest of the city which mirror one another, Oesterheld constructs a counterpoint which fences in most of the Buenos Aires capital district. Waste spaces are, in this film, very far from 'insignificant'.

Postscript: the letter 'ñ' is also itself marginalised, treated as *ñiquiñaque* by digital globalised communications where it upsets character strings

Figure Ñ.1 Martín Oesterheld, still from *La multitud* (Buenos Aires, 2012). Courtesy of the director.

and gets displaced from keyboards, and banned for proper names in France only a few years ago, yet reclaimed as key to Spanish-speaking and Breton culture by its users.[10]

Notes

1. Our translation. Real Academia Española, 'ñiquiñaque', in *Diccionario de la lengua española*, 23.4 ed. <https://dle.rae.es> [accessed 26 November 2020].
2. Sigmund Freud, 'The Uncanny' [1919], in *The Standard Edition of the Complete Psychological Works of Sigmund Freud, XVII (1917–1919): An Infantile Neurosis and Other Works*, ed. by James Strachey and Anna Freud (The Hogarth Press and the Institute of Psychoanalysis, 1955), pp. 217–52.
3. *La multitud*, dir. by Martin Oesterheld (J. C. Fisner, 2013).
4. Cristian Silva, 'The interstitial spaces of urban sprawl: Unpacking the marginal suburban geography of Santiago de Chile', in *Creative Spaces: Urban culture and marginality in Latin America*, ed. by Niall Geraghty and Adriana Laura Massidda (Institute of Latin American Studies, 2019), pp. 55–84.
5. *Natura Urbana: The Brachen of Berlin*, dir. by Matthew Gandy (UK/Germany, 2017).
6. Silva, 'The interstitial spaces of urban sprawl', p. 55.
7. Italics in the original. Freud, 'The Uncanny', p. 241.
8. Freud, 'The Uncanny', p. 226 and pp. 241–4.
9. Niall Geraghty and Adriana Laura Massidda, 'The spatiality of desire in Martin Oesterheld's La Multitud and Luis Ortega's Dromómanos', in *Creative Spaces: Urban culture and marginality in Latin America*, ed. by Niall Geraghty and Adriana Laura Massidda (Institute of Latin American Studies, 2019), pp. 201–39.
10. AFP, 'French baby boy banned from having name containing tilde', *The Guardian*, 13 September 2017, <https://www.theguardian.com/lifeandstyle/2017/sep/13/french-baby-boy-banned-from-getting-name-containing-symbol> [accessed 15 June 2021].

Outsourcing

Matthijs de Bruijne

Figure O.0 Nina Mathijsen, *Collage O*, 2021. © takeadetour.eu. Courtesy of the artist.

Hats, toys, medicines, make-up, reading glasses, gloves, underwear, used syringes, spoons, pens, backpacks, suitcases, keys, telephones, shoes, newspapers, trousers, bibles, cuddly bears and endless umbrellas. Every day, train cleaners come across these objects during their shift. Some objects end up at the Lost and Found department; most end up in a waste container.

Before the Dutch state started in the 1990s to reform its public utilities into market-oriented companies, a train cleaner worked for Dutch Railways for only a few years before being promoted to conductor or train driver. After the privatisation of this transport company in 1995, cleaners' work was outsourced and this type of ladder disappeared; once a cleaner, always a cleaner. During the first years after privatisation, Dutch Railways played cleaning companies off against each other, driving the price of outsourced work down and down. Therefore, cleaning had to be done faster until 90 seconds to clean a train toilet became the reality. Dutch Railways did not assume responsibility for this squeeze. Privatisation meant companies could flush their social responsibility down the drain. The work and the worker became exchangeable and invisible. While passengers sleep, outsourced workers remove the objects left behind in trains. In the morning, passengers board a clean train without realising who has done the work.

But not only had the cleaners' work become invisible to train passengers, their union had also disappeared from view. The need for change was great but the trade union was not able to unite this group of outsourced workers, who worked harder and harder. Their old union structures were useless: mostly white male shop stewards no longer represented the new group of cleaners, who were mostly women and migrants. The Dutch Union of Cleaners, FNV, realised that only by organising the union differently could they succeed. They began to change, in terms of organising model, from a bureaucratic apparatus to a movement from the bottom up; in the long run, the cleaners became once again the protagonists of their trade union.

In 2010, cleaners in the Netherlands started a national strike for better working conditions. It was remarkable that this strike was not so much directed against workers' employers as against the companies that hired them. As trash piled up on trains, the work of the cleaners was made visible again. Surprisingly, passengers showed an extremely high level of understanding for the strike despite travelling on what had become effectively waste bins: more 'off the rails' than on them! Perhaps, I speculate, this understanding came from a shared experience in a

Figure O.1 Matthijs de Bruijne, *Union of Cleaners FNV in Brussels*, 4 April 2014. Courtesy of the artist.

context of increased outsourcing in many sectors, so that cleaners were not the only ones under ever-increasing pressure.

The strike lasted longer than any other strike in the Netherlands since the 1930s. After three months the cleaning companies, and above all their clients, understood that they had lost the strike. The cleaners achieved their first victory, which proved to be a turning point for those in poorly paid, outsourced jobs. Since that year, the cleaners' slogan, 'Nooit meer onzichtbaar!' ('Never again invisible!'), has continued to resound in the Netherlands.

Problem

Bruno Vindrola-Padrós and Ulrike Sommer

Figure P.0 Nina Mathijsen, *Collage P*, 2021. © takeadetour.eu. Courtesy of the artist.

The imminent threat of overflowing material remains has been posited as one of the most evident crises of the Anthropocene. As the urge to conceal and abolish waste strengthens, we turn to technological research and development for a solution. However, to paraphrase Pierre Bourdieu and Loïc Wacquant, the crucial task for the social researcher is not to quickly align towards a solution, but firstly to understand why this problem has been officially considered worthy of being studied and how it has been framed.[1] In other words, what are the historical conditions leading to our consideration of waste as a problem?

The last two decades of 'waste studies' in the environmental and social sciences have shed some light on this history. The idea of a crisis of waste accumulation, while fairly recent,[2] is in fact enmeshed in a long history: of industrial activity (mass production and technological development) and 'destructive' consumption,[3] of the modern categorisation of dirt and cleanliness (the invisibilisation of dead bodies, human substances, broken objects, that are considered 'dirty'), and of the inequalities consolidated in the (post)colonial world (where countries from the 'Global South' are faced with consequences due to waste accumulation originating from industrialised nations). On a deeper level, the 'waste crisis' is also the result of the particular history of Western thought, wherein technology, which would come to be regarded as the essence of knowledge,[4] was fundamentally concerned with turning matter into useful objects.[5] It is in modern times that this philosophy of human technical mastery over nature,[6] and its distaste for the 'useless', becomes dominant.

The (historically constituted) urge to remove waste from sight in our contemporary world, while at the same time not hesitating to keep producing it, just enhances our incapacity to understand it.[7] *Homo faber* unavoidably transgresses the principle of utility at the same time as professing it. In other words, in the historical drive towards technology, development and mass production, industrialised nations have foregone their capacity to understand 'waste' as a social category and a concrete materiality. Waste signals the limits of knowledge,[8] or rather, the limitations of our ways of constructing knowledge. It remains a problem under the gaze of the current technocratic regime in its obsession with maximising the economic utility of things. It would seem, then, that the waste crisis is an epistemological crisis.

The past, as an endless source of epistemes, a repository of different ways of knowing from societies of different times and places, gives us perspective. Some of these epistemes are long lost; others can

Figure P.1 Bruno Vindrola-Padrós, *The everyday pottery sherds at the Early Neolithic Criş settlement of Tăşnad Sere (Satu Mare, Romania)*, 26 July 2016. Courtesy of the author.

become intelligible with careful consideration. For instance, consider the different understanding of waste in the Balkan Neolithic. From approximately 7000 BCE, the Balkan peninsula witnessed an unprecedented accumulation of material remains. We observe this from 'tell' sites: settlements where built structures are constructed one on top of the other over time (as distinct from 'flat' settlements). These populations lived very closely with pottery remains that would nowadays be simply considered 'waste'.[9] Potsherds were not merely dumped, as in modern urban landfills, but integrated in social life, whether as tools and artefacts in various crafts and food-processing activities, body ornaments, markers of domestic spaces or constituents of ovens and possibly floors. It would have been inconceivable to live without these things. Thus, the practical knowledge of what to do with these broken objects was fundamental. This different form of knowledge and regime of waste simply expose the fact that waste as we know it is a relative and historical category,[10] a by-product of capitalism. Similarly, the waste crisis as a 'problem' forces us to remember that knowledge need not be constructed as the attempt to control the 'natural' world for the sake of economic utility.

Notes

1. Pierre Bourdieu & Loïc Wacquant, *An Invitation to Reflexive Sociology* (University of Chicago Press, 1992), p. 236.
2. Gay Hawkins, *The Ethics of Waste* (Rowman & Littlefield, 2006), p. ix.
3. David Graeber, 'Consumption', *Current Anthropology* 52 (2011), pp. 489–511, p. 492.
4. Max Horkheimer & Theodor W. Adorno, *Dialectics of Enlightenment* (Stanford University Press, 2002), p. 2.
5. Tim Ingold, *The Perception of the Environment: Essays on livelihood, dwelling and skill* (Routledge, 2000), p. 298.
6. Guy Schaffer, 'Camp', in *Discard Studies Compendium*, 2010, <https://discardstudies.com/discard-studies-compendium/#Camp> [accessed 15 June 2021].
7. Michael Shanks, David Platt & William L. Rathje, 'The perfume of garbage: Modernity and the archaeological', *Modernism/Modernity* 11 (2004), pp. 61–83, pp. 64–66.
8. Barry Allen, 'The ethical artifact', in *Trash*, ed. by John Knechtel (MIT Press, 2007), pp. 198–213, p. 206.
9. Bruno Vindrola-Padrós, *The Early Neolithic Broken World: The role of pottery breakage in central and southeastern Europe* (unpublished doctoral thesis, UCL, 2020).
10. Theodor M. Bardmann, 'Wenn aus Arbeit Abfall wird – Überlegungen zur Umorientierung der industriesoziogischen Sichtweise', *Zeitschrift für Soziologie* 19 (1990), pp. 179–94, p. 190.

Queer liveliness/Queer matter/Queer toxin

Mel Y. Chen

Figure Q.0 Nina Mathijsen, *Collage Q*, 2021. © takeadetour.eu. Courtesy of the artist.

Listen to the climate change discourse. Along with claiming ecological harm, it will also casually say that some populations, understood as singular, enumerable, and imaginable as segregated species – it's all in a name, after all – are in peril. These populations are imagined as reliant, at their core, on their reproductivity; their reproductivity, at *its* core, is reliant on a narrow imagination of single-species sexual reproduction and generational survival. Too easily have binary genders, allied with other binarisms, attached to these poignant imaginations: contradictions between normalcy and precarity that further secure efforts to banish the strange or aleatory. They are the carriers of climate value. This is just one reason that queerness of gender, sexuality or embodiment is thought to coconspire with toxicity. It's all too easy: a toxin is a radically undesirable quantity. It appears to threaten death. Yet toxins are simultaneously life. They are life in several ways. Their agitative bent suggests a kind of liveliness, a vivid animation among other things. In their introjection, such as in the form of a vaccine, they also attenuate their own threatening nature by a feat of mimicry: like shan't destroy like, and a life may be spared. But what is rarely considered by the larger whole is how the figuration of a queer as toxic to the life of others figures as a toxin to the life of the queer. Judgments are relative. The trick of the queer toxin is to make the wrong matter matter, and to turn it into life where there seemed none, or to death where there seemed too much; to reinvest matter where it seemed wasted; and to undo waste *and* life such that survival requires not the movement of the very earth but a recognition of what has been there all along. This is a circular form of thought. You have been exposed, but you already knew this.

Rubble

Adam Przywara

Figure R.0 Nina Mathijsen, *Collage R*, 2021. © takeadetour.eu. Courtesy of the artist.

Rubble (Latin: *rudus*; French: *débris*) is a matter which sets a material and metaphorical limit to the traditionally conceived object of a ruin. Rubble is found at sites where the life cycle of a building has come to an end and the last wall has come crashing down, be it a countryside house, an urban tenement block or a monumental cathedral. Rubble defies categorisation, appearing as a territory of heterogeneous fragments where destitute building materials mix with soil and hardly recognisable traces of human endeavour start to disappear under ruderal plant species. The state of abandonment and destitution can easily deceive our perceptions of both the agency and the history behind such landscapes. Deemed detritus, rubble is too easily assigned the role of historical *leftover*, and therefore left out of narratives about our culture.

In contemporary anthropological scholarship, the idea of rubble has been scrutinised, and redefined as a textured and socially entangled matter; as such, 'rubble' contrasts with the cunning abstraction of a 'ruin'. The latter, as anthropologist Gastón Gordillo has shown in the postcolonial context of Argentina's Gran Chaco, is a conceptual tool forged in modernity to allow a definite temporal distinction beneficial for the ruling classes: 'The pastness of the past is crystallized in efforts to present ruins as objects separated from the present.'[1] However, as Ann Laura Stoler suggested in her editorial to the volume *Imperial Debris*, this temporal distinction collapses as soon as we consider the material and immaterial outcomes of ruination as results of 'colonial processes that entangle people, soil and things'.[2] The resulting conceptual framework necessitates a reassessment of the temporality of both rubble and ruins in order to grasp how 'imperial formations persist in their material debris, in ruined landscapes and through the social ruination of people's lives'.[3] The lens of ruination that I use here, drawing on these sources and specific contexts, reintroduces rubble as one persistent material witness to past violence, whether of colonialism, extraction or war.

Historian Tony Judt points out that during World War II, the 'full force of the modern European State was mobilized [...] for the primary purpose of conquering and exploiting other Europeans'.[4] Processes of colonial ruination were unleashed on the continent, and particularly its eastern fringes. Central to that emergent geography of ruination was Poland, where six years of German occupation caused social, environmental and material destruction on a historically unprecedented scale. The occupier targeted the daily life of the country, disrupting it as well as the spaces and symbols around which it revolved. A particular example of that politics of ruination became the capital city of Poland. Warsaw, a densely populated urban environment of 1,200,000 people in 1939, was by 1945 transformed through a multistage process of destruction into a desert of rubble and ruin, almost uninhabited except by ruderal species and ruderal social forms.

In the wake of war, the images of Warsaw's ruins were showcased nationally and internationally through government news channels as evidence of German barbarity. In the 1950s, the same images were juxtaposed with photographs of the reconstructed city, legitimising the 'miracle' of Polish reconstruction. Yet, behind that irrefutable visual evidence, which entered historical books and shaped historical narratives, a crucial historical experience of the period was lost. An experience of a whole generation of people, of a ruderal society, which *lived with* the rubble, inhabiting the ruins, clearing salvaged bricks and searching and reworking rubble in order to survive. An estimated 20,000,000 cubic metres of rubble was touched, turned, moved and transformed in post-war Warsaw. The process, which lasted almost a decade, entangled politicians, architects and the mass of labourers recruited from across the society. Many of those labouring on the rubble had been torn out by the war – like rubble from buildings – from their familiar social and economic structures. In large majority, this social group was formed of women, called 'abandoned' since their relatives had been killed or remained lost to the war. These women, working in the cold winter months, without proper clothes and tools, laid the groundwork for rebuilding architectural and social life in Warsaw. And they shared the historical trajectory of the rubble that in the post-war years became embedded in the Warsaw landscapes and architecture, inasmuch as they have effectively disappeared from historical consciousness.

Notes

1 Gastón Gordillo, *Rubble: The afterlife of destruction* (Duke University Press, 2014), p. 2.
2 Ann Laura Stoler, ed., *Imperial Debris: On ruins and ruination* (Duke University Press, 2013), p. x.
3 Stoler, *Imperial Debris*, p. 10.
4 Tony Judt, *Postwar: A history of Europe since 1945* (Random House, 2011), p. 14.

Space junk

Alice Gorman

Figure S.0 Nina Mathijsen, *Collage S*, 2021. © takeadetour.eu. Courtesy of the artist.

Figure S.1   NASA, *Energy flash when a projectile launched at speeds up to 17,000 mph impacts a solid surface at the Hypervelocity Ballistic Range at NASA's Ames Research Centre*, Mountain View, California, 1963. Copyleft.

Space junk consists of all the discarded rockets, satellites and objects launched into space by humans, and the fragments and dust that result from their decay in the harsh space environment. It also includes some sparse biological remains from animals, insects and plants. Usually space junk refers to human-manufactured materials in Earth orbit. There are, however, abandoned human artefacts throughout the solar system.

In Earth orbit, space junk is moving fast – on average 7 to 8 km/s. This means collisions can cause damage. A piece of junk can pierce a satellite's shell, smash its solar panels or cause it to explode into a cloud of even more space junk spinning at high speed. Explosions also happen when leftover fuel in rocket bodies becomes unstable. Spacecraft regularly have to move out of the way of approaching space junk to avoid collision. Although it has been recognised since the 1970s that increasing amounts of debris could make orbital space unsafe and inaccessible, as yet there are no proven mechanisms to get rid of old debris.

When discarded, space junk may be boosted high into a graveyard orbit, or sent to hell literally on Earth: plunging through the thick

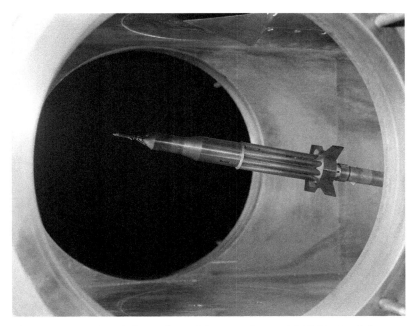

Figure S.2 NASA, *Wind tunnel test of Saturn rocket model*, 1962. Copyleft.

atmosphere to burn. At low altitudes, space junk is eventually dragged back into the atmosphere, but large quantities remain in orbit at higher altitudes above 2,000 km.

Spacecraft resemble chimerical insects, their exoskeletons shielding the delicate neurons of electronic circuitry, their entrails composed of fuel systems with stainless steel stomachs filled with nourishing fluids like hydrazine (which is toxic to humans). Their rigid bodies are adorned with antennas, solar vane wings, camera eyes, Dalek limbs and protuberances. While living, they speak to robots on Earth and to each other, relaying disembodied voices, images and data over the range of the electromagnetic spectrum. Sometimes, satellites are discarded and cut off from human contact before their own voices cease. These spacecraft hover between life and death, dark shadows haunting orbit. Some have compared old satellites to zombies as they stalk the living satellites through the dim corridors of space.

The swarm of space junk forms a sort of non-biological ecology. Microbes are represented by small particles and dust, like the famed flecks of paint from the US Space Shuttles. At the top of the food chain are highly evolved spacecraft, such as the European Space Agency's

Envisat. Launched in 2002, it is now considered one of the most dangerous pieces of junk due to its large size and location. At the moment, there are no natural predators, so the junk is accumulating and spiralling out of control. It is up to humans to create robot predators and so introduce balance to this new ecology.

Time and Tower: Grenfell

José Torero Cullen

Figure T.0 Nina Mathijsen, *Collage T*, 2021. © takeadetour.eu. Courtesy of the artist.

Why is time so fundamental to the link between space and waste? Between an initial spark and a catastrophic conflagration, there is time; between the occupant's recognition of danger and safety, there is time; between a building that protects us and one which harms us, there is time. Between a living space and a waste ruin, there is, once again, time. In this time, in this interval between the spark and the inferno, we can fight and control the fire and we can bring ourselves to safety. We can prevent the waste of lives and the wasting of the building. Conscious decisions involved in the creation of the places in which we live, congregate and work define the literally vital relationship between fire and time.

The time is midnight, 14 June 2017, and the place is Grenfell Tower in London. Almost three hundred people, seeking rest at the end of a long, hot summer day, were being sheltered by the tower. A small kitchen fire started on the fourth floor of the building. By sunrise, 72 occupants had lost their lives. The building envelope that had been intended to give them shelter had, in fact, altered the course of time and irreversibly changed the lives of many. A tower like Grenfell, or many others, can be a community, can provide shelter, can enable sustainability and can mean efficiency and the minimisation of waste. But a tower also challenges the relationship between fire and time. It takes a long time to bring people out of a tower, and fire, helped by buoyancy, can spread upwards rapidly. Thus a tower, if not managed correctly, can mean life being wasted.

Society has created a regulatory framework, a social contract, that guarantees that a fire will not challenge the safety of those who call the tower home. It is the tower that is meant to protect its occupants by not allowing the fire to spread. The occupants can 'stay put' ('stay-put' strategy), confident that the tower will protect them. In Grenfell, the building envelope changed the relationship between fire and time by allowing the fire to spread at a rate that drastically reduced the time available for the occupants to evacuate and for the firefighters to respond. For those who could not respond faster than the fire, time stopped.

Why did time stop at Grenfell? The tower was supposed to contain the fire so that occupants could safely stay put, but instead of providing time, it eliminated it. But equally: why did time run so fast at Grenfell? Instead of delivering the time necessary to enable those trapped to be rescued, it accelerated destruction, hampering those who were meant to rescue. So, why was there, all of a sudden, no more time for so many people to continue to live their lives? Have we built a space where we no longer understand the relationship between fire and time?

Underground

Luke Bennett

Figure U.0 Nina Mathijsen, *Collage U*, 2021. © takeadetour.eu. Courtesy of the artist.

Whether in the form of commodious basements, impervious subterranean shelters or vast waste repositories, the underground offers up a promise of voluminous service to our storage, shelter and disposal needs. But the underground is a trickster, as likely to spit out as to swallow the matter and life injected into it.

Letting go of most unwanted things on Earth will – by action of gravity alone – see them fall to the ground. Here they will lie, either decaying into the ground or helping – through their stubborn refusal to break down – to form part of a new sedimented layer, by which the ground slowly rises beneath our feet, turning successive layers of former surface into *underground*. This seeming ability of the ground to swallow waste matter into itself, and to carry it down into an out-of-sight and out-of-mind underground, has long been exploited for waste disposal. Following the Industrial Revolution, and the burgeoning volumes and varieties of intractable wastes to be got rid of, via the rise first of coal power (ashes) and then of petrochemicals (plastics), the 'pushing' of waste into the underground became the dominant form of waste disposal. This accelerated, intentional, human-authored deposition and undergrounding of our discarded useless matter is one hallmark of the Anthropocene. In the United Kingdom, an abundance of worked-out mining and quarry voids provided ample (and cheap) opportunity for an accelerated undergrounding of layers of municipal and industrial wastes, and until prohibited by the EU's Landfill Directive, enacted in

Figure U.1 Nicole Clouston, *Microbial growth in mud from Lake Ontario Portrait*, 2018. Courtesy of the artist.

1999, the UK's landfills were designed on the principle of 'dilute and disperse'.[1] These were not to be secure containment cells, but rather accelerated *insertions* into the ground: matter emplaced there with the explicit aim that it would quickly meld with its surroundings, and continue that onward, gravity-assisted journey away from human sight and attention, into the underground.

But just as (for 'depth' psychologists like Freud or Jung)[2] the burial of unwanted feelings or experiences runs the risk of a sudden, and unexpected, traumatic reverberation, so the undergrounding of wastes can see painful, unwanted, revenant effects. Thus, methane gas and leachate emanating from waste's decay can break out from their underground confinement, visiting their poisonous effects upon the surface. Meanwhile, seemingly stable 'made ground' can, over time, slump or fissure, as its underlying extractive voids (now filled in) settle, in turn unsettling both the ground above and our convenient imaginings of the underground as an accepting, passive, sponge-like receptacle. This troublesome quality is also to be found in our other appropriation of the underground, as a promise of shelter for our precious possessions (think of underground vaults, crypts, tombs and buried treasure) and even for shelter of our vulnerable living, fleshy bodies in times of crisis (think of improvised underground air-raid shelters, fortified subterranean bunkers).[3] But this sheltering is contingent, because the underground is ultimately not a safe place for either our possessions or our bodies. Just as the underground can push back against waste injected into it, so the atmospheric conditions of the underground corrode, compress and entrap, and the distinction between a shelter and a tomb lies only in the question of a viable route of escape back to the surface. Whether through the lens of revenant waste or in glimpsing the smothering, life-stifling peril of underground dwelling, we come to see that the underground is never fully under our control.

Notes

1 Alistair Allen, 'Containment landfills: The myth of sustainability', *Engineering Geology* 60 (2001), pp. 3–19 (p. 12).
2 Sigmund Freud, *Civilisation and its Discontents* (Penguin Books, 2004 [1930]); Carl Jung, 'Mind and Earth', in *The Collected Works of C.G. Jung, Volume 10: Civilization in Transition*, ed. by Herbert Read et al. (Routledge and Kegan Paul, 1964 [1927]), pp. 45–69.
3 Luke Bennett, 'The Bunker: Metaphor, materiality and management', *Culture & Organization* 17 (2011), 155–73.

Vastus

Véra Ehrenstein

Figure V.0 Nina Mathijsen, *Collage V*, 2021. © takeadetour.eu. Courtesy of the artist.

In 2020, two major scientific journals, *Nature* and *Science*, drew their readers' attention to the fate of tropical forests in a warming climate.[1] A hundred scientists were warning the world that the ability of old-growth, structurally intact rainforests to act as carbon sinks, and to sequester ever more CO_2 through photosynthesis, is weakening. Higher rates of tree mortality, which could be heat-related, might account for the diminishing metabolic uptake. Scientists project that in a warmer climate that affects hydrological cycles, some parts of the Amazon could even turn into non-forest ecosystems.[2] Were these ecosystems to change so much that they switched from being a carbon sink to being a carbon source, this would increase the already high carbon losses caused by clearing, forest fires and logging, and would thereby add to the CO_2 emissions from the relentless burning of fossil fuels and further exacerbate global warming.

These worrying findings about the carbon-storage properties of tropical forests are based on data collected in hundreds of research plots located across South America, central Africa and south-east Asia. Often located in national parks, vegetation patches situated within the confines of these plots are assumed to be shielded from direct human disturbance. One might think of such places through the keyword *vastus*, the Latin term for 'unoccupied' or 'uncultivated', usually associated with ideas of unproductivity, uselessness and an unrealised potential. This keyword raises the question of what (who and how) makes the value of tropical forests, now a threatened carbon sink. In addition to scientific data, lush ecosystems in protected areas provide a wilderness experience to tourists, thus drawing their economic value from being currently unpopulated (*vastus*). Yet state-of-the-art ecological knowledge indicates that the biological fabric of seemingly pristine forests often bears the marks of past cultivation activities (not so *vastus* after all). Scientists working in west and central Africa recently circulated a call to pay closer attention to forest histories, and to read supposedly intact vegetation as 'an archive of the slave trade, conflicts, diseases and depopulations that left farm and village lands abandoned'.[3] It is important to acknowledge the material traces of socio-natural pasts in order to develop historically aware environmental ethics, as well as to rethink what it means to manage these 'legacy forests'[4] sustainably once they are reconceived as 'haunted landscapes' of the Anthropocene.[5]

Various policy mechanisms and regulatory initiatives targeting tropical forests have developed in the last decade that rely on the quantification of the forests' metabolic functions but ignore their other uses.[6] One example is the reforestation and conservation projects set up to produce and sell emissions offsets indexed on how much CO_2 planted or protected trees are sequestering. Another development is the multiplication of bilateral result-based deals whereby overseas aid is used to reward reduced deforestation and associated carbon removals. The government of Norway has made a few such deals, notably with Brazil,

Indonesia and Gabon. Lastly, voluntary sustainability standards for commodities such as palm oil now include requirements regarding the non-conversion of 'high carbon stock' vegetation. The revaluation of tropical forests through a climatic lens creates new wastelands: degraded forests,[7] or even grassy savannas,[8] that must be (re)afforested, restored or developed; if they do not provide enough carbon storage, then they should sustain highly productive crops, certainly not be left unattended – so the story goes. There is a craze these days for tree planting and forest protection, driven by proliferating carbon metrics, framed within an economised logic and its tyranny of usefulness. A telling example is the controversial 'global tree restoration potential' study that maps where trees could be added across the Earth's terrestrial surface and estimates the quantity of additional carbon stored.[9] Funded by big philanthropic money, the study has been aggressively advertised (and swiftly criticised for its scientific flaws), illustrating another tyranny, that of 'impact' at all costs. Obsessions with usefulness have had highly detrimental consequences in the past, on people (think of the frantic yet not so successful *mise en valeur* of the French colonies), other living beings and our planet – so why not try to revalue the *vastus* for what it is: the unproductive, unrealised, undeveloped, which, well, just exists?

Notes

1 Wannes Hubau et al., 'Asynchronous carbon sink saturation in African and Amazonian tropical forests', *Nature* 579 (2020), 80–7; Martin J. P. Sullivan et al., 'Long-term thermal sensitivity of Earth's tropical forests', *Science* 368 (2020), 869–74.
2 Thomas E. Lovejoy and Carlos Nobre, 'Amazon tipping point', *Science Advances* 4 (2018).
3 Gretchen Walters et al., 'Deciphering African tropical forest dynamics in the Anthropocene: How social and historical sciences can elucidate forest cover change and inform forest management', *Anthropocene* 27 (2019), 100214.
4 Walters et al., 'Deciphering African tropical forest dynamics in the Anthropocene'.
5 *Arts of Living on a Damaged Planet: Ghosts and monsters of the Anthropocene*, ed. by Anna Tsing et al. (University of Minnesota Press, 2017).
6 Vera Ehrenstein, 'Carbon sink geopolitics', *Economy and Society* 47 (2018), 162–86.
7 Jenny E. Goldstein, 'The afterlives of degraded tropical forests: New value for conservation and development', *Environment and Society* 5 (2014), 124–40.
8 William J. Bond et al., 'The trouble with trees: Afforestation plans for Africa', *Trends in Ecology & Evolution* 34 (2019), 963–5.
9 Jean-Francois Bastin et al., 'The global tree restoration potential', *Science* 365 (2019), 76–9; Aisling Irwin, 'The everything mapper', *Nature* 573 (2019), 478–81.

Wasteland

Miranda Griffin

Figure W.0 Nina Mathijsen, *Collage W*, 2021. © takeadetour.eu. Courtesy of the artist.

wasteland: *noun*, an abandoned or deserted territory.

The unfinished twelfth-century romance by Chrétien de Troyes, *Le Conte du Graal* (the *Tale of the Grail*),[1] is the first to tell the tale of the naïve knight Perceval. As he is instructed in the ways of chivalry, Perceval is told that a good knight must not speak too much. Journeying through the Arthurian landscape, Perceval is welcomed to the opulently appointed castle of a wounded king, where he witnesses a mystical procession of handsome youths and beautiful maidens bearing strange objects including a grail (understood at this point as a large dish). The young knight longs to understand this extraordinary spectacle: what is the grail for, he wonders, and, more specifically, whom does it serve? But he remembers his instructions and stays silent. When he wakes the next morning, the castle is deserted: as his adventures continue, however, Perceval is confronted by characters who reproach him for his failure to ask whom the grail serves (they use this terminology insistently, seemingly omniscient about what Perceval wanted to say but never did). Because of Perceval's failure, the wounded king remains incapacitated and the land is deserted.

The wasteland is revisited throughout Arthurian literature of the Middle Ages. In some versions, the land is not just damaged, it is almost erased. In the strange and sprawling work *Perlesvaus*, composed a few decades after the *Conte du Graal*, the failure of the eponymous knight to

Figure W.1 *Perceval à la Recluserie*, Bibliothèque Nationale de France, BNF Richelieu Manuscrits Français 111, fol. 244v, Quête du saint Graal, France, Poitiers, XVe siècle. Courtesy Bibliothèque Nationale de France.

ask the question makes the land impossible to navigate or understand: strange pits and fissures appear in the earth; knights lose their way, and when they meet each other they are bound to fight to the death instead of observing the chivalric rules of mercy and honour.

The wasteland, then, makes a powerful connection between human speech and the natural world. It is a devastation wrought by a choice to follow instruction rather than intuition, by a fear of voicing curiosity and concern. It is a wasted space, created as the result of a wasted opportunity: the result of a rigid protocol that prescribes silence rather than curiosity as a response to strange, troubling scenes or practices.

But while the knight who fails to ask the question is reminded constantly of his error, these reminders give him and his companions the opportunity to try again and again. Chrétien's Perceval never comes back to the castle and never asks the question, but as the tale is taken up by new authors, Perceval and other knights rediscover the castle, circling the answer but never quite finding it out.

In the various versions of the tale, it's unclear whether the land is devastated by the missing question, or whether the failure to ask simply means that the wasteland remains unhealed. In other words, there might be just one opportunity to ask the question, or an infinite series of moments to do so. Perhaps at a time when we are facing extinctions and climate chaos, it's already too late to ask questions to halt the devastation of the landscapes we inhabit. But should that stop us asking?

Note

1 Chrétien de Troyes, *The Complete Story of the Grail: Chrétien de Troyes' Perceval and its continuations*, trans. Nigel Bryant (D. S. Brewer, 2015).

Xenophobia

Huda Tayob

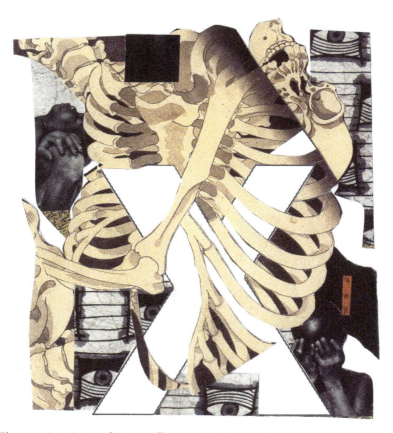

Figure X.0   Nina Mathijsen, *Collage X*, 2021. © takeadetour.eu. Courtesy of the artist.

xeno- /ˈzɛnəʊ/ *combining form* relating to a foreigner or foreigners; other, different in origin;[1] alien, strange, guest.[2]

Last train to Kinshasa, last train to Kinshasa …

It was 2015, and I was talking to Anthony, a Zimbabwean activist and refugee, in the city centre of Cape Town. It was a hot, dry day and we met in the Cape Town public library, sheltering from the sun in the cool nineteenth-century interiors. Over the past few months, while collaborating on research, we had spoken frequently about the damaging effects of xenophobic violence in Cape Town, violence often called Afro-phobia as it particularly targets Black Africans from other parts of the continent. On this January afternoon, Anthony was recounting his own experience of Cape Town in 2008, when xenophobic violence spread throughout South Africa during the winter months of May and June. He had fled to South Africa with his family in 2003 to escape political violence in Zimbabwe. He spoke of the weight of fear, before moving to South Africa in 2003, and then the uncanny and unexpected recurrence during the winter of 2008. At the time, he was staying in Imizamo Yethu township in Cape Town, where he was an active community member and school teacher. He described the unexpected blow of having his home looted and burnt, of leaving in a hurry never to return. He spoke of mistrust, growing suspicions and a heightened feeling of foreignness after 2008; of some South Africans who protected his family, and others who threatened his children. Being marked as 'foreign' in South Africa has meant being a disposable Black body and nothing more, like many others. Yet midway in our conversation, while talking about the constant fear and feeling of being alien and strange, he described his experience a few days earlier at Salt River railway station in Cape Town.

It was an early evening, and he was taking the last train home, to Bellville – the area in Cape Town he had moved to following the violent displacement of 2008. Bellville had offered a temporary safe haven to many people like Anthony fleeing violence, and continues to be a longer-term space of refuge. As he was rushing to board the train to Bellville, the conductor called out 'last train to Kinshasa, last train to Kinshasa …'; that was his train. As Anthony recounted, the conductor had referred to the same suburb the previous week as 'little Mogadishu'.

Perhaps this is what xenophobia does: it combines the meaning of Cape Town with Kinshasa and Mogadishu, a strange and alien new construct formed in part by an apartheid history of modernist Whiteness, post-apartheid urban violence, and the streets of some, any, African city. These are cities untethered from their countries, displaced.

'Mogadishu' and 'Kinshasa' are standing in here for somewhere else, some place Black and African. These are places associated with dirt and waste, marked by failure and the detritus of history. The naming and calling out evokes the dark underbelly of xenophobic violence that resurfaces periodically in South African cities, which demarcates those darker African cousins as superfluous, available to be discarded. As Françoise Vergès reminds us, there is a long history of black and brown bodies, made disposable and superfluous, as waste. She writes, 'The word "waste" usually refers to rubbish, but it is important also to consider the phrase "laying waste". Slavery, colonialism and capitalism have laid waste to lands and people.'[3] This is an anti-Blackness encoded into how the nation and home operate, and the very language and grammar of belonging.[4] Postcolonial states have not been immune to this structure.

For Anthony, the conductor's shifting terminology was a reminder that he and many others were visibly identifiable as not belonging, as darker-skinned; a reminder of previous threats and violent events. It was a reminder that 'Bellville' has come to mean a foreign space, part of the African continent associated with dirt and informality, in contrast to the pristine beauty of Cape Town 'proper'. Yet Bellville, for Anthony, is also the space of refuge and safety formed in the wake of xenophobic violence. Refuge is a complex space. Fiston Mwanza Mujila reminds us in his novel *Tram 83*, writing of an unnamed African city, that 'our trains have lost all sense of time',[5] and we might add here, perhaps they have lost their sense of place too. Yet, while recalling the extractive and colonial practices associated with railways across the African continent, Mujila also remembers that there might be a glimmer of another world in these spaces too, for 'according to the fickle but ever-recurring legend, the seeds of all resistance movements, all wars of liberation, sprouted at the station, between two locomotives'.[6]

Notes

1   Based on entry in *Oxford Dictionary of English* (3rd edn), ed. by Angus Stevenson (Oxford University Press, 2011–; online version available through Oxford Reference).
2   Meaning drawn from *Collins English Dictionary*, <https://www.collinsdictionary.com/dictionary/english> [accessed 6 January 2022].
3   Françoise Vergès, 'Capitalocene, waste, race, and gender', *e-flux* 100 (2019), <https://www.e-flux.com/journal/100/269165/capitalocene-waste-race-and-gender> [accessed 15 June 2021].
4   Kathryn Yusoff, *A Billion Black Anthropocenes or None* (University of Minnesota Press, 2018).
5   Fiston Mwanza Mujila, *Tram 83* (Deep Vellum Publishing, 2016), p. 1.
6   Mujila, *Tram 83*, p. 1.

Yawning and Yearning for elsewheres and for the right to stay

Tatiana Thieme

Figure Y.0 Nina Mathijsen, *Collage Y*, 2021. © takeadetour.eu. Courtesy of the artist.

Yawning is a spontaneous bodily expression of ambivalence. It can be read as fatigue, boredom and the liminal phase between states of stillness and movement. A yawn can also be an adaptive response to and reconciliation with the need to wait and exercise a 'politics of patience' in the face of constant 'threats to life and space' at the urban margins.[1] *Yearning* can be a sentimental call to another time and place that seem far away and inaccessible, but it is not a reconciliation with that distance. Rather, it is a form of persistence, that must decide whether to give in to melancholia or retain a measure of hope that a return to that place and time might be possible, or that conversely the right to stay in the present place will come, even if this place can never be home. Yawning and Yearning can occur simultaneously – as the embodied affirmation of both exhaustion and resistance. A yawn is also a yearn for more oxygen, for the expanded capacity to breathe.

Christina Sharpe's *In the Wake: On Blackness and being* interrogates the everyday representations of Black life in North America in the 'afterlife' of slavery, reflected in the continuous forms of 'non/status' and criminalisation of Black bodies.[2] Extending this reflection beyond the shores of the Americas to evoke the historical and present-day manifestations of the trans-Atlantic slave trade, colonialism and racial capitalism, she describes the bodies 'transmigrating the African continent toward the Mediterranean and then to Europe who are imagined as insects, swarms, vectors of disease, familiar narratives of danger and disaster that attach to our always already weaponized Black bodies (the weapon of blackness)'.[3] In the last chapter of her book, Sharpe explores the violent ecologies of what she calls the *weather*, an assemblage of environmental pressures on vulnerable bodies in motion and transience. The cold, the wind, urban pollution, over-policing …

In Porte de la Chapelle, Paris, tired bodies huddled under a bridge in the winter of 2018, yawning while holding their breath against the pollution and police evacuations. Yearning for peace, for a space to stay for more than one night at a time. Yearning for a day when the idea of tomorrow wasn't filled with impossibility and more waiting. Grassroots activists standing not far from the bridge set up tables and started buttering rolls. They too were dishevelled, but they were not hiding. They vented, smoked, verbally trashed the government for its growing criminalisation of migrants and those trying to assist them. They exhaled smoke and inhaled the car fumes, flicked cigarette butts to the curb, went back into the warehouse to get more supplies and heat up the coffee urn. By day, these pavements became the stage of DIY humanitarian solidarities and distributions;[4] by night they turned into zones of exposure to the cold, hard drugs and sleeping rough. The spaces under and around bridges offered ephemeral and tenuous refuge for migrants who had no place to go but no legal right to stay (yet).[5]

As spontaneous archaeological sites of makeshift shelter, at dawn, the night's temporary materials for warmth and rough sleeping became the day's relics of municipal disorder and civic disapproval. The pavements and spaces under the bridge formed a tapestry of humanitarian remains from the days prior – empty cups, blankets left behind, cigarette butts. And amongst the material refuse, these tired bodies displaced by conflict or the violence of economic poverty were themselves bodies 'out of place',[6] at risk of yet another potential police evacuation.

Yawning and yearning, their bodies moved, stood and waited,[7] from street-based hubs of hanging about to standing in queues and waiting rooms, at the edges of either asylum or expulsion, in what Sharpe calls a 'plunge into unbelonging'.[8] They waited for the queue to form across the street where volunteers set up the daily breakfast distribution so these mostly young male migrants in asylum limbo might have a cup of coffee and a buttered roll. They waited for their appointment at the prefecture, for a court date, for their papers.

The queues and the hanging-about hubs have now splintered or moved elsewhere. Some of these migrants were able to endure the lengthy asylum procedures and asserted their 'politics of presence'[9] in the city – making home and work, shaping diverse forms of participation in *their* Paris life world. These migrants might be classified as 'new Europeans'.[10] Other migrants continued to sleep rough under the bridges, either leaving Paris when the permanence of waiting became unbearable or getting sucked into the crack-smoking community on the '*colline du crack*' near Boulevard Ney. This Paris is the city of *yawns*, where bodies have huddled and stood or run away 'in absence of country',[11] displaced but having arrived at no place. This is the Paris where tired bodies *yearn* for breath, whether in hiding, in the queue or at the hands of police. This Paris is invisible and yet it too is present and in full view.

Notes

1 Arjun Appadurai, 'Deep democracy: Urban governmentality and the horizon of politics', *Environment and Urbanisation* 13 (2001), pp. 23–44, p. 30.
2 Christina Sharpe, *In the Wake: On Blackness and being* (Duke University Press, 2016), p. 16.
3 Sharpe, *In the Wake*, p. 16.

4   Kavita Ramakrishnan & Tatiana A. Thieme, 'Peripheral humanitarianism: Ephemerality, experimentation, and effects of refugee provisioning in Paris', *Environment and Planning D: Society and Space*, 40:5 (2022), pp. 763–85.
5   Tatiana Thieme, Eszter Krasznai Kovacs & Kavita Ramakrishnan, 'Refugees as new Europeans, and the fragile line between crisis and solidarity', *Journal of the British Academy* 8 (2020), pp. 19–25.
6   Mary Douglas, *Purity and Danger: An analysis of concepts of pollution and taboo* (Praeger, 1966).
7   Cathryn Brun, 'Active waiting and changing hopes: Toward a time perspective on protracted displacement', *Social Analysis* 59 (2015), pp. 19–37.
8   Sharpe, *In the Wake*, p. 107.
9   Jonathan Darling, 'Forced migration and the city: Irregularity, informality, and the politics of presence', *Progress in Human Geography* 41:2 (2016), pp. 178–98.
10 Here I'm echoing the *National Geographic* October 2016 issue, which featured a cover story titled 'The New Europeans: How waves of immigrants are reshaping a continent', pp. 83–115.
11 Sharpe, *In the Wake*, p. 107.

Zero waste

Pushpa Arabindoo

Figure Z.0 Nina Mathijsen, *Collage Z*, 2021. © takeadetour.eu. Courtesy of the artist.

zero waste, *noun*, a situation in which no waste material is produced

zero-waste, *adjective* (also zero waste), not producing any waste material

In December 2018, the planning group of Zero Waste International Alliance adopted an updated, peer-reviewed and internationally accepted definition of 'zero waste' as '[t]he conservation of all resources by means of responsible production, consumption, reuse, and recovery of products, packaging and materials without burning and with no discharges to land, water or air that threaten the environment or human health'.[1] Aligning with the guiding principles of a zero-waste hierarchy that goes beyond recycling, reusing and reducing to rethinking and redesigning product consumption as a top priority, its pithy, globally accessible doctrine-style statement is comparable to popular definitions of 'zero waste' such as that by the *Cambridge English Dictionary* cited above.

And yet, can zero-waste calls for eliminating waste be plainly interpreted as 'no waste', as these definitions suggest, lay or scientific? Can such a profound and important idea requiring a remarkable investment of sociopolitical change really be that simple? In non-mathematical contexts, 'zero' might seem synonymous with or even a more emphatic alternative to 'no'. But as linguistic scholars would argue, 'zero' as a numeral is semantically and pragmatically distinct from 'no' as a generalised quantifier. So, if zero waste cannot be interpreted as no waste, what does it imply? Are we referring here to a kind of net zero, where waste generated is somehow eradicated (albeit sustainably)? Or to a more entrepreneurial possibility of waste neutrality, offsetting it by whatever means to balance its generation? If it is about making waste disappear, then, in all likelihood, this is done by moving it elsewhere, not by eliminating it. Also, can we talk about the eradication of waste when, under the continued capitalist influence of reformist ideals, this ignores the economic vitality of waste as a resource (of a different kind) to millions of informal waste pickers around the world, particularly in the Global South?

What is the intended meaning of 'zero waste', and how can we interrogate it, beyond the obvious? We can perhaps start by asking what the purpose is of adding 'zero' to 'waste', as this odd conjugation poses a double problematic. For, instead of the dialectical synthesis one might expect, the two terms problematise each other – zero's cardinality of counting and ordinality gained by ordering and placing zero first is compromised by its nominal or a namesake attachment to the problem of waste, while waste as a problem is hardly resolved by the invocation of zero as a fetishised solution. They are both caught in a teleological fix wherein these two great modern inventions risk being bound by a narrow conception of limit, ignoring zero's nuanced bridging of the finite and the infinite as well as waste's materiality, which is more indeterminate than determinate. Thus, a zero totality is a notion that does not assume the numeric and is undefined, but in being indefinitely degenerate, that is, infinitely capable of reinterpretation, it renders the nonzero state undesirable. Any statistical noise that zero makes in this context vis-à-vis waste stems from a consolidation of aggregate measures that will struggle to be a justifiable basis for strong empirical claims.

While zero waste definitely addresses an ontological reality, whether it provides new kinds of epistemological insights is uncertain when you consider that both metonymy and metaphor are at work in its often crude knowing. Thus, the etymology of the term 'waste', which is derived from the Latin *vastus*, meaning 'unoccupied or desolate', suggests a lack which might, in a raw sense, equate to zero value. Caught between the semantic of a metonym and a figurative reading of a metaphor, what we are left with is a contingency where a synecdochical reading of zero waste creates a discomfort around its discursive consequences, exposing it as rhetorical and making a critical reading of zero waste even more urgent.

Note

1   Zero Waste International Alliance, 'Zero waste definition', 2018, <https://zwia.org/zero-waste-definition/> [accessed 29 October 2022].

⁎: Corona shapes

Albert Brenchat-Aguilar

Figure ⁎.0 Nina Mathijsen, *Collage ⁎*, 2021. © takeadetour.eu. Courtesy of the artist.

An asterisk in a text signals something marginal: fringeworthy, for afterwards, shrunken, willingly unseen, it might be the emblem of many human lives. Furthermore, the asterisk that heads the present text is serifed and thereby somehow queer, with each tip weirdly protruding and exaggerated, softened and imparting a sense of movement: features that do not contribute to the symbol's legibility and may even detract from it, increasing its marginality. This queer asterisk, I suggest, may also be considered an image of the virus SARS-CoV-2, its tips paradoxically both animated – due to their capacity to assemble with the environment – and de-animated, life-sucking, lethal.[1] It is the dreaded combination of excessive liveliness with death-dealing that fits those matters of waste: from the decaying matter, biohazards and toxic e-waste to the wayward, anxious, threatened, abandoned, oppressed humans that deal with waste matters while being treated as waste.

Beginning in March 2020 and for a hundred days thereafter, curator and historian Chus Martínez posted one story a night on her Instagram account, thus accompanying many of us during the UK's first lockdown. Under the title *CORONA TALES*, each of her histories was headed by one of the many computerised images of coronaviruses that were increasingly populating news outlets and social media (Figure *.1). In such images, SARS-CoV-2 was fictionalised as a simple, reproducible, fixed entity composed of a spherical core, preferably rough-surfaced, from which extend elongated spines each tipped with a swollen protuberance. Such simplified images of SARS-CoV-2, developed in response to the combined didactic intentions of biologists, illustrators and the media, I shall refer to as 'corona shapes', placing them alongside the queer asterisk as manifestations of our fears and fantasies.[2]

The corona shapes presented in the media have little by little ingrained themselves into our Gestalt perception, penetrating our capacity to differentiate between familiar shapes in three different ways. First, corona shapes have blended with the environment, whether by acquiring the textural qualities of surrounding objects or by forming patterned structures that themselves become a kind of environment – see, for example, the designs incorporating corona shapes by Ghana Textiles Printing, which build on the Ghanaian tradition of memorialising significant events in textiles.[3] Second, the corona shape in isolation brings into intimate contact previously unconnected objects such as pin cushions, pomander balls (homely Christmas oranges stuck with cloves), *Pilea peperomioides* (the 'money plant') and, indeed, the engorged asterisk. Newly bubbled as 'corona shapes', these and similar objects are infected with a new significance. Third and finally, the corona

Figure *.1 Chus Martínez, *Corona Tales*, 2020; collage by Albert Brenchat-Aguilar. © Ana Domínguez. Courtesy of the artist.

shape has been absorbed into images of the human body, producing queer embodiments of the viral identities that have accompanied racist, sexist, classist and ageist media representations.[4]

Video games such as Minecraft quickly adapted, offering not only avatars that wear protective suits and masks but also virtual skins that render human heads as corona shapes (some animated to change shape constantly).[5] I offer as a striking realisation of the new environment the animated illustration by Eduardo Navarro that Chus Martínez chose as the cover image of her December 2020 open letter (Figure *.2). The naked (or clothed skin-tight) humanoid figure turns its face towards us and smiles in a welcoming, playful gesture. Its posture is contorted: one hand on a hip, the other coquettishly laid where a human might have a cheek. The legs are apart, the body turned away from us, hiding physical characteristics that might indicate sex. The animation both invites and withholds a contact that the past year have warned us is potentially deadly. Dangerously, one of the figure's hands touches its circular face, the surface of the virus. The tongue-tip pokes out, getting closer to its own viral skin, which expands and gains fleshiness in the animated version, where the spikes rhythmically protrude and retract. In line with

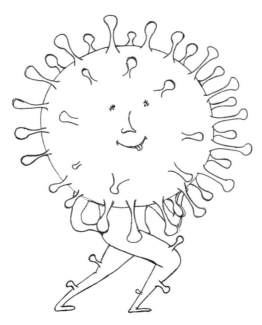

Figure *.2 Eduardo Navarro, *Untitled*, 2020; animation: Esther Hunziker (see https://espaciofronterizo.com/borderland/animated-skins-part1/). © Eduardo Navarro. Courtesy of the artist.

media exhortations over the past years the injunction 'don't touch' is here intimately entangled with that to 'look closely'. Navarro's figure is another embodiment of the human–viral hybrid represented also by Minecraft's avatars – and by the queer asterisk.

Skin is a primary feature of all these representations – it is the heart (so to speak, but on the outside, the periphery) of the corona shape. The virus's skin is presented as hybrid and frightening, ever present in both its capacity to attach to our cells and its vulnerability to soap or sanitiser. Meanwhile, the media reported stories of 'skin hunger': a desire for human touch that is explained as a biological need.[6] It has long been thought that haptic communication affects human stress, infants' wellbeing and adolescents' behaviour;[7] even our immunity, pain, and attention levels depend on touch.[8] A year of the coronavirus pandemic was enough for researchers to publish papers assessing the health of touch-deprived people.[9] Touch deprivation, however, must be understood in interaction with class and professional differences: the elderly person, forced to isolate in the home or care home, where what history will call senicide has taken place, is both contrasted with and dependent on the key worker – the cleaner, delivery rider or nurse – who is exposed more than ever to touching human and non-human viral surfaces. The transformation of human touch into a sort of dangerous but desired fetish will no doubt endure in human relational habits as well as in the imagery through which we approach the world and other people.

In our and the virus's approach to the environment, queered, peripheral, asterisked lives are at stake: those that are overly homed or un-homed, insecure, facing deportation, outside the protective social skins that might have helped them survive. It is a hostile environment that has rendered certain sectors of society more vulnerable than any virus could ever have imagined (if a virus could be conscious). When we see corona shapes as human asterisks/asterisked humans, we understand the identification that has been achieved between the equally vulnerable human and viral skins, blending bodies with the environment, matters of waste with bodies treated as waste of our socio-economic constructions.

Notes

1 Mel Y. Chen, *Animacies: Biopolitics, racial mattering, and queer affect* (Duke University Press, 2012).
2 I highlight the work of David Godsell who, having drawn viruses and bacteria for many years, capitalised upon his work during the pandemic. However, his complex drawings and

animations were simplified to the extent that a static image of the virus ended up spreading through the media. See some of his pre-Covid work at: Jon Cohen, 'Meet the scientist painter who turns deadly viruses into beautiful works of art', *Science*, 11 April 2019 <https://www.sciencemag.org/news/2019/04/meet-scientist-painter-who-turns-deadly-viruses-beautiful-works-art> [accessed 3 April 2021].

3   Ama de-Graft Aikins & Bernard Akoi-Jackson, '"Colonial virus": COVID-19, creative arts and public health communication in Ghana', *Ghana Medical Journal* 54:4 Supplement (2020), pp. 86–96 <https://doi.org/10.4314/gmj.v54i4s.13>.

4   Beyond overtly racist references to 'yellow peril' in various forms, which triggered defence campaigns such as #ImNotAVirus and #EndTheVirusOfRacism, the media have perpetuated viral identities through unconscious bias. In the interest of image representation in this paper, I highlight the British East and South East Asian Network reporting that 'Out of 14k images pulled from various UK news outlets reporting on COVID-19, 33% of a sampled subset were found to have images of ESEAs unnecessarily'. Generally, intersectional identities – specifically, in the UK, older Black and Latinx working-class female key workers – have been useful to describe categories of vulnerabilised subjects.

5   NameMC, 'Coronavirus minecraft skins', <https://namemc.com/minecraft-skins/tag/coronavirus> [accessed 3 April 2021].

6   Sirin Kale, 'Skin hunger helps explain your desperate longing for human touch', *Wired UK*, 29 April 2020, <https://www.wired.co.uk/article/skin-hunger-coronavirus-human-touch> [accessed 28 September 2020].

7   T. Field, 'American adolescents touch each other less and are more aggressive toward their peers as compared with French adolescents', *Adolescence* 34:136 (1999), pp. 753–8.

8   Miller School of Medicine, *Touch Research Institute (Archives)* <https://med.miami.edu/centers-,-a-,-institutes/mailman-center/community/other-community-based-programs/touch-research-institute-(archives)> [accessed 30 December 2022].

9   Joanne Durkin, Debra Jackson & Kim Usher, 'Touch in times of COVID-19: Touch hunger hurts', *Journal of Clinical Nursing*, 30:1–2 (2021), pp. e4–e5, <https://doi.org/10.1111/jocn.15488>.

1%

Andreas Philippopoulos-Mihalopoulos

Figure 1.0 Nina Mathijsen, *Collage 1*, 2021. © takeadetour.eu. Courtesy of the artist.

You know how we all like to hate the 1%? That sliver of society representing the richest and filthiest of them all? Those scoundrels who splutteringly consume capitalist caviar while discharging mounds of colonial excreta? And scoundrels they are. They tick most of the clichés of gender, class, skin colour and especially geographical location, and they own more than half of the world's wealth, as established by the now infamous Credit Suisse global wealth report.[1]

But they are not 'they'. They are not some distant beasts. Pronoun confession moment: they is *we*. *We*, the Londoners, the Europeans, the Global North. We who consider ourselves literate, artistic, sensitive, cultured. We who consider ourselves ecologists. We: the 1%.[2] Think about it: there are bound to be 99 other people in the world worse off than every person we know, including ourselves. That's all it takes to be part of this exclusive club.

And that shit surrounding us, it's all ours. Let's own up to our pronouns.

We are all complicit.[3]

We are all children of the Anthropocene, comfortable with pollution, extractivism and excretisation, as long as our lifestyles continue with only cosmetic changes – a bit of karma-caressing recycling here, a touch of rustic composting there. And if anyone were to visit the Earth from elsewhere, they would be forgiven for thinking that waste production was our actual mission. Waste production has become not only an end in itself but, as Baudrillard argues, politically generative of Western capitalism: waste appears as 'the essential function, the extra degree of expenditure, superfluity, the ritual uselessness of "expenditure for nothing" becoming the site of production of values, difference and meanings on both the individual and the social level'.[4] The production of waste rather than goods has become the disavowed but unerring indicator of abundance, affluence and social pre-eminence.

But our ingeniousness stretches further: we manage *not* to drown in our own seepage. We send it away, sailing it across the indelible routes of inhuman and excremental colonialism that have shaped this tilted, bitter Earth. Flush it away, out of sight. Haphazardly covered up in the North, our waste proliferates across the landscapes of the Global South.

Yet, as Baudrillard announces, 'there are no longer any dustbins'.[5] What we flush returns to haunt us, a hyperobject of fractal omnipresence.[6] Our air is filling with data waste, our dreams and our bodies become pixelated microplastic dioramas. The barbarians have reached the gates; their stench threatens to overcome our smelling salts. And there is nowhere to send them, nowhere to hide them – or ourselves. 'We' have now become 'it': not only are we 'submerged by the waste-products of industrial and urban concentration, but ... we ourselves are transformed into residues'.[7]

Figure 1.1 Andreas Philippopoulos-Mihalopoulos, *Oceans of Eternity V: Contract unto extinction*, at K.U.K. gallery, Trondheim, Norway, on 6 September 2022. Photograph by Melchior Blum. Courtesy of the author.

Show us your trash and we will award you your exclusive 1% Club card.

We are all complicit.

In this whirl of excretal individualism, we do not operate alone. We find partners in crime. We form collective bodies that leak uncontrollably our desire for more-more-more. Oh yes, we are part of the 'flat ontology': we proclaim that all bodies human and nonhuman share the same plane of immanence. Oh yes, we cannot discriminate ontologically: we are *all* subjects and objects of the same patterns, norms, laws. This is the *lawscape*, as I have called it elsewhere – the tautology between law and matter.[8] The lawscape is indeed flat, partly following post-Deleuzian new materialist understandings of how human and nonhuman bodies have the same claim to existence and indeed absence of value judgment differentiation.[9] But significantly, it is also unequal. Its flatness is tilted. Weightier bodies pull it down. Our 1% Club is perhaps the weightiest of all. It brings us together (while keeping us apart) in bourgeois individualism, the ideology grounding our legal and political universes – universes that our barium-infused defecations topple, whatever efforts for a cleaner planet might be happening elsewhere.[10]

Ladies and gentlemen, we regret to inform you that the Club's toilets are blocked.

We are all complicit.

Notes

1. Credit Suisse, *Global Wealth Report*, <https://www.credit-suisse.com/about-us/en/reports-research/global-wealth-report.html> [accessed 20 January 2022].
2. Jill Treanor, 'Half of world's wealth now in hands of 1% of population – report', *The Guardian*, 13 October 2015, <https://www.theguardian.com/money/2015/oct/13/half-world-wealth-in-hands-population-inequality-report> [accessed 20 January 2022].
3. In its repetition, this is an incantation I have used in my art practice and specifically my performance practice. See Andreas Philippopoulos-Mihalopoulos, 'We are all complicit: Performing law and water', in *Laws of the Sea*, ed. by Irus Braverman (Routledge, 2022), pp. 282–93. The term is drawn from Reza Negarestani, *Cyclonopedia: Complicity with anonymous materials* (re-press, 2008).
4. Jean Baudrillard, *The Consumer Society: Myths and structures* (Sage, 1998), p. 43.
5. Jean Baudrillard, *The Illusion of the End* (Polity Press, 1994), p. 26.
6. Timothy Morton, *Hyperobjects: Philosophy and ecology after the end of the world* (University of Minnesota Press, 2013).
7. Baudrillard, *The Illusion of the End*, p. 78.
8. Andreas Philippopoulos-Mihalopoulos, *Spatial Justice: Body lawscape atmosphere* (Routledge, 2015).
9. See, for example, the excellent blog by Levi Bryant, one of the main proponents of flat ontology, at <https://larvalsubjects.wordpress.com/2010/02/24/flat-ontology-2/> [accessed 20 January 2022].
10. Oxfam International, 'Carbon emissions of richest 1 percent more than double the emissions of the poorest half of humanity', 21 September 2020, <https://www.oxfam.org/en/press-releases/carbon-emissions-richest-1-percent-more-double-emissions-poorest-half-humanity> [accessed 20 January 2022].

HS2

Chia-Lin Chen

Figure 2.0 Nina Mathijsen, *Collage 2*, 2021. © takeadetour.eu. Courtesy of the artist.

HS2 (i.e. High Speed 2), the British government's project to 'level up' the neglected north of England 'with over 250 miles of new high-speed line', is in trouble.[1] Although the project has received cross-party support,[2] its escalating costs, route change and partial cancellation have cast doubts on the government's commitment.[3] Raising environmental and wildlife concerns, the organisation HS2 Rebellion[4] describes it as 'the most expensive, wasteful and destructive project in British history'. Opponents reject official justifications for this costly investment and contest the economic benefits it will supposedly bring by rebalancing regional polarisation. Ironising on famous names that express high-speed modernity, such as the Japanese 'bullet train' or the world's fastest steam train, the *Mallard*, HS2 sceptics advocate scrapping this 'inflated white elephant'.[5] Despite these doubts, supporters of HS2 argue that investment in new rail infrastructure is overdue: the rail network has been exploited for over 150 years, serving freight and passengers on both long-haul inter-city and commuting metropolitan/regional services, and has now reached capacity. HS1 (formerly the Channel Tunnel Rail Link, and covering only 107 km) is the sole newly built rail link in over a century; moreover, it meets growing demand only around London and parts of the southeast.[6] 'Rebalancing Britain' is a key governmental aim underlying HS2 investment. Strategic master plans exploiting new rail hub positions are proposed for areas with HS2 stations, whereby wastelands in urban cores are projected to become vibrant urban centres.

Could the French experience be prophetic for the controversial HS2 project?

The French TGV (Train à Grande Vitesse) celebrated its 40th anniversary in September 2021. Its success has eradicated doubts, led to long-term development of the network and addressed the over-dominance of Paris and its surrounding area. The regional cities of Lyon and Lille have flourished, showing how strategic location of high-speed rail stations in wastelands near city centres can integrate urban regeneration and assist regional revitalisation. Few people today recall that the TGV was not always considered a far-sighted transport intervention, but faced decades of opposition. The TGV was initially an unwanted child, conceived by France's national state-owned railway company (SNCF) and inspired by the Japanese Shinkansen bullet train. In spite of the common impression that the French love grand projects, many government officials, as well as local communities, politicians and environmentalists, opposed the project. The economic cost was seen as alarming and unjustified by what was perceived as a prestige project for businessmen. Environmental opponents argued that the TGV would disrupt wildlife and nature (ecological systems destroyed, farmlands lost) and built environments (local communities' NIMBY claims: Not In My Back Yard).[7] François Mitterrand, leader of the parliamentary opposition through much of the planning period, claimed that 'TGV is only going to cause headaches and will do nothing for our [territory]'.[8]

Perhaps the most surprising opponent was the national planning agency (DATAR), responsible for regional development policies, which considered that the hub-and-spoke shape of the TGV network would depopulate the countryside and reinforce, rather than reduce, the dominance of Paris. In the 1960s, when the environmental movement was still in its infancy and the future for rail dubious due to competition from car and air travel, DATAR favoured building roads, considering that the rural countryside was better served by motor traffic. The SNCF insisted that the planned TGV route would minimise disruption, and that the train would ultimately be an environmental ally, saving energy and reducing pollution. But without the coincidence of various international and domestic events – notably the 1973 oil crisis and rail financial crisis and the need for modernisation – plans for the TGV would probably have failed.

Today the TGV is valued in France, and its technology has been adopted in various countries. Its success has revitalised the struggling rail system. Evidence from the past 40 years indicates that, instead of focusing on Paris, the TGV has facilitated socioeconomic benefits and functional arrangements among TGV cities. Major regional cities have been boosted, even if not all cities have had the same results. This success has not had an entirely smooth course, and has required substantial extra work. Every TGV line has faced difficulties in the planning and implementation stages. The ongoing Bordeaux–Toulouse TGV project has been seriously delayed, awaiting reconciliation among differing interests and actors. Multi-level interventions, leadership and integrated strategic planning by proactive regional governments have contributed crucially to the success of the TGV-Nord network in revitalising wider subregions beyond regional centres in the Nord-Pas-de-Calais region.

The UK and France share the challenges arising from regional polarisation and dominant capital cities. The French experience demonstrates that a new high-speed rail network could bring a renewed socioeconomic dynamism that would help develop regional cities. However, the history of the TGV shows us also that wider regional revitalisation is never automatic or universal. In the post-pandemic, zero-carbon future, the success of the HS2 project will depend crucially on strategic planning and proactive actions taken in response to the challenges that its implementation throws up. Clearly, HS2 on its own is insufficient. For the UK, renowned for its incremental and muddling-through approach to mega-infrastructure, the process looks likely to be long. But the optimistic view maintains that, with integrated and strategic planning guided by clear vision, claims for the wider benefits of HS2 may well be justified.

Notes

1. High Speed Two, <https://www.hs2.org.uk/> [accessed 30 October 2022].
2. High Speed Two, *HS2: Realising the potential* (UK Government, 2018), <https://assets.hs2.org.uk/wp-content/uploads/2018/07/17154802/22403_Realising_the_potential_WEB.pdf> [accessed 30 October 2022].
3. Department for Transport, *Integrated Rail Plan for the North and Midlands* (UK Government, November 2021), <https://assets.publishing.service.gov.uk/government/uploads/system/uploads/attachment_data/file/1062157/integrated-rail-plan-for-the-north-and-midlands-web-version.pdf> [accessed 30 October 2022].
4. HS2 Rebellion, <https://www.hs2rebellion.earth/> [accessed 30 October 2022].
5. Scott Murphy, 'HS2: Cheshire MP calls on government to scrap "white elephant"', *Northwich & Winsford Guardian*, 11 June 2022, <https://www.northwichguardian.co.uk/news/20201354.hs2-tatton-mp-calls-government-scrap-white-elephant/> [accessed 30 October 2022].
6. High Speed One, <https://highspeed1.co.uk/> [accessed 30 October 2022].
7. See Jacob Meunier, *On the Fast Track: French railway modernization and the origins of the TGV 1944–1983* (Praeger, 2002).
8. Meunier, *On the Fast Track*.

From 3rd world to included 3rds: designs for living

Lucy Bell

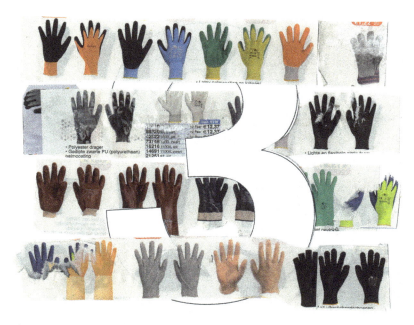

Figure 3.0 Nina Mathijsen, *Collage 3*, 2021. © takeadetour.eu. Courtesy of the artist.

Modern capitalism is built on a binary opposition between 'useful' and 'wasted' lives: between those who serve the capitalist system and those excluded from it.[1] Given the strong connections between social and material processes, it is no surprise that those living 'wasted' lives also often live with, on and off waste. Vast communities live in sprawling informal settlements built from repurposed materials, in houses at the edges of municipal landfill sites, and make a living by waste-picking.[2] These communities are only heard above the noise of the global media through fleeting news flashes: homeless waste-picker shot dead by military police in São Paulo (2017); tragic landslide kills 116 at Koshe landfill in Addis Ababa (2017); 246 confirmed dead in landslides across Rio de Janeiro's flooded favelas (2010). When they make it through the noise, they are a chilling reminder of a massive design failure: one that, far from being a simple issue of urban design, is founded on centuries-old systems of exclusion constructed on intersecting categories of race, class and gender.

Capitalist, colonial modernity was built on hierarchies carefully arranged by European man to place himself at the top and all others below him, in descending order of power and privilege. At the bottom of the pyramid is 'the Third World': a term coined by French geographer Alfred Sauvy in 1952 in the context of the Cold War. In spite of Sauvy's anti-imperial intentions, the term has come to emblematise the inferiority, otherness and backwardness of huge populations and environments – principally in the Global South – as seen from and in the interests of the West.[3] As Arturo Escobar so forcefully theorises, global capitalism's dependence on the false hierarchies and binary or ternary relations conceived by a tiny human minority is a 'massive design error'.[4] This error on a cosmic scale has led to extractivism, exploitation, slavery, genocide, the Anthropocene and the imminent possibility of our extinction as a species.

As COP26 made so blatant, our global society urgently needs to adopt alternative forms of living, being and thinking. Listening to and learning from the 'others' that this massive design error has created – those whose lives are treated as waste – offers us hope in how it allows us to reconceive of the 'third'. The former 'Third World', in part by *virtue* of its being excluded from the 'banquet' of Western modernity,[5] offers a plethora of voices articulating points of departure for a wasteless design: migrants, refugees, asylum seekers, homeless people, waste-pickers, prisoners and Indigenous communities.

I highlight here just two examples from Latin America of communities who embody and theorise, in the present, alternative futures based not on a hierarchically organised one-world political ontology but a pluriverse premised on a praxis of horizontality and inclusion. Best known are the Zapatistas, who fight for and model a 'world where many worlds fit', and whose 2021 counter-insurrection in Europe gave countless communities and organisations the chance to learn from their struggle.[6] Similar but different are the *Ch'ixinakax utxiwa*. As Silvia Rivera Cusicanqui argues, the limited political recognition granted by the Bolivian state to these mixed-heritage Bolivians 'converts them into minorities, ensnaring them in indigenist stereotypes of the noble savage and as guardians of nature'.[7] This mode of identification and categorisation gives them what Rivera Cusicanqui calls 'residual status' – that is, the reduction to an inferior, peripheral social standing, to a form of societal 'waste'. Rivera Cusicanqui offers instead the notion of *ch'ixi*, which expresses 'the Aymara idea of something that is and is not at the same time. … A *ch'ixi* color gray is white but is not white at the same time; it is both white and its opposite, black.' In short, *ch'ixi* 'is the logic of the *included third*'.[8] This complex Aymara concept of subtle differentiation is crucially different from that of hybridity as theorised by Néstor García Canclini, which Rivera Cusicanqui rejects via the biological example of the mule: the merger of two different beings produces a sterile third.[9] Contrastingly, the Aymara concept of *ch'ixi* allows for a muddling or intermingling of different elements that are never fully mixed, and which allow for reproduction with variation. The implication, when thinking about the mixing of different identities, subjectivities, ontologies, cultures and cosmologies, is that differentiation and heteronomy can occur without producing binary oppositions and supernumerary thirds, and, indeed, without the need to generate something 'completely new' – a need that characterises our culture of capitalism, consumerism and of course, waste.

So, let's finish with an alternative design for the number 3. Not an *excluded third world* – whose peoples are relegated to subhuman status by the all-powerful white male-dominated state – but rather a *world of included thirds*, whose motley mixes of humans and other-than-humans are all invited. In this world of many worlds, wasted beings and environments are not even a possibility, because there is space for all those that do not fit, for those that exceed reductive binaries, for those who are and are not at the same time.

Or rather, let's start again by exploring some playful pathways into *a world of included thirds*. Such passages are being designed, opened up and walked every day in Latin America, in and by communities and at the grassroots. Take for example the fascinating world of *editoriales cartoneras* – cartonera publishers who make books out of discarded cardboard collected from the streets to amplify the voices and disseminate the stories of communities facing conditions of marginalisation, stigmatisation and violence.[10] Whether working

Figure 3.1 *Cartonera books.* Photograph by Vassilis Korkas, 2016. Courtesy of the artist.

with waste-pickers in the cases of Eloísa Cartonera (Argentina) and Dulcinéia Cartonera (Brazil), Indigenous communities and languages in the cases of La Cartonera (Mexico) and Yiyi Jambo Cartonera (Brazil/Paraguay), or imprisoned men and women in the cases of Colectiva Editorial Las Hermanas en la Sombra, La Rueda Cartonera and Viento Cartonero (Mexico), these publishers open up plural worlds through the very logic of the *included third*. Their motley collectives and colourful books scream out thanks to powerful encounters across deeply flawed yet inflexible social barriers, and through narratives that refuse to dilute differences or what we might call – following Marisol de la Cadena and Mario Blaser's pluriversal concept of the 'uncommons'[11] – uncommonalities.

Notes

1. Zygmunt Bauman, *Wasted Lives: Modernity and its outcasts* (Polity, 2003).
2. Lucy Bell, 'Place, people and processes in waste theory: A Global South critique', *Cultural Studies* 33:1 (2019), pp. 98–121.
3. Vicky Randall, 'Using and abusing the concept of the Third World: Geopolitics and the comparative political study of development and underdevelopment', *Third World Quarterly* 25:1 (2004), pp. 41–53.
4. Arturo Escobar, *Designs for the Pluriverse: Radical interdependence, autonomy, and the making of worlds* (Duke University Press, 2018), p. 33.

5 Alfonso Reyes, 'Notas sobre la inteligencia americana', in *Latinoamérica: Cuadernos de cultura latinoamericana,* 15 (1976 [1936]) pp. 5–12, p. 5.
6 Franca Marquardt, 'The Zapatistas' "Journey for Life" and its implications for a global solidarity', *Convivial Thinking*, 2 December 2021, <https://convivialthinking.org/index.php/2021/12/02/the-zapatistas-journey-for-life/> [accessed 11 November 2022].
7 Silvia Rivera Cusicanqui, 'Ch'ixinakax utxiwa: A reflection on the practices and discourses of decolonization', *South Atlantic Quarterly* 111:1 (2012), pp. 95–109, p. 99.
8 Rivera Cusicanqui, 'Ch'ixinakax utxiwa', p. 105. My emphasis.
9 Rivera Cusicanqui, 'Ch'ixinakax utxiwa', p. 105.
10 Lucy Bell, Alex Flynn & Patrick O'Hare, *Taking Form, Making Worlds: Cartonera publishers in Latin America* (University of Texas Press, 2022).
11 Marisol de la Cadena & Mario Blaser, eds., *A World of Many Worlds* (Duke University Press, 2018).

4th Industrial Revolution and 6th extinction: Post-Anthropocene

Everisto Benyera

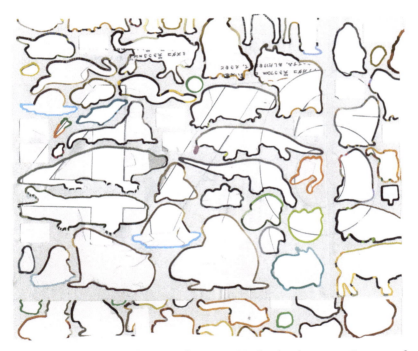

Figure 4/6.0 Nina Mathijsen, *Collage 4*, 2021. © takeadetour.eu. Courtesy of the artist.

In *The Fourth Industrial Revolution and the Recolonisation of Africa*, I argue that the looting of Africa that started with human capital and natural resources now continues via the looting of data and digital resources, leaving a harmful wake of waste behind.[1] Developing the notion of 'coloniality of data', I posit that the Fourth Industrial Revolution (4IR) is the final phase, which will conclude Africa's peregrination towards recolonisation. The connection between the digital revolution and recolonisation replicates the colonial origins of the Anthropocene and its disproportionate taxation on Africa. This conjunction also accelerates the 6th global extinction.

The 4IR is a massive systemic shift in the way people live, work and relate. It was caused by the many advances in technology and the resulting merge of nanotechnology, biotechnology, robotics, networked digital computation, and information communication technology, among others. Taken together, these technological developments blur the traditional boundaries between the physical, the digital, the sentient and the biological worlds. The 4IR is a significant accelerator of the 6th mass extinction of life on this planet. Also known as the Holocene extinction or the Anthropocene extinction, this is a period of extinctions caused by the great acceleration of human activities, but coming to a crescendo due to the environmental impact of inventions framed under the 4IR. Requiring ever more extraction on a finite, exhausted planet, the technological inventions of the 4IR are the greatest agencies of death and extinction.

The 4IR is a culmination of the multiplier effect of the past three industrial revolutions, one resulting in multiple wastes: epistemic, material, social, ethical, ideological, existential and so on. Machines that were novel in the third industrial revolution are obsolete and reduced to waste in the 4IR. While there is understandable focus on technology-related waste, there is also non-technological waste precipitated by the 4IR. I will list six types of such waste as a way of showing how the 4IR accumulates wasted lives on the African continent.

1. A vulnerable *humanity* classified as the 'digi-deprived' will be excluded from the realms of humanity. Without a digital footprint, the digi-deprived will be technologically invisible and become extinct. This digital divide will expand, as robots, transhumans, cyborgs and other forms of 'enhanced' humanity populate the world.
2. Cultural boundaries and forms of collective identity will be 'wasted' as allegiances shift to software technology. *The family, kinship*, consanguinities and human relations will be replaced with digital connections such as social media followers, likes and online groups.
3. *National borders*, ironically fixed in earlier rounds of African colonisation, will wane as the new connected communities

will transcend territoriality and reside in borderless cyber-geographies. State sovereignty will erode and the locus of authority will shift to the emerging tech oligarchy and multinational corporations.
4. *Workers*, especially those doing manual labour, will become obsolete and be replaced by robots. After all, robots do not complain, nor do they strike and demand salary increases, get sick or take smoke breaks. Labour will disappear with the synchronisation between the physical factory floor and the cyber computational space.
5. *Ethical human decision-making* will be 'wasted' and replaced by artificial intelligence (AI) and digital algorithms, which are faster, sharper, scientific and more accurate in achieving measurable outcomes.
6. Lastly, the *physical empire* will be 'wasted' and replaced by the cognitive empire, which invades humanity's mental space. The new emperor will be the tech companies, and the new mantra 'hail the algorithm'.

Note

1 Everisto Benyera, *The Fourth Industrial Revolution and the Recolonisation of Africa: The coloniality of data* (Routledge, 2021); Everisto Benyera (ed.), *Africa and the Fourth Industrial Revolution: Curse or cure?* (Springer, 2022).

5G

Sy Taffel

Figure 5.0 Nina Mathijsen, *Collage 5*, 2021. © takeadetour.eu. Courtesy of the artist.

5G is the standard for wireless mobile telecommunications that succeeds the 4G, 3G, 2G and 1G systems. 5G affords significant increases in the bandwidth available for cellular connections and reduces latency between wirelessly connected devices. It may seem counterintuitive to find technology such as 5G listed within this *Wastiary*; waste is typically assumed to be material that has reached the end of its useful existence and is consequently discarded. 5G, on the other hand, is new, 'cutting-edge', 'innovative' digital technology. Rather than existing within the cultural imaginary as obsolescent waste, alongside 'dead media'[1] such as VHS tapes, audio-cassettes and 16-bit video game cartridges, 5G is a future-facing technology whose benefits are not meaningfully experienced by many today, but which enables continued rapid growth in mobile data traffic and connection speeds in the future. This common-sense perspective on the relationship between technology and waste is characterised by a flawed understanding of the materiality of early twenty-first-century digital technologies, particularly regarding the spectacular volume of waste produced during every stage of their life cycle.

This materiality is obscured by the longstanding discursive framing of digital technology as 'post-industrial', 'knowledge-based', 'informational', 'immaterial' and 'virtual'.[2] Collectively this framing suggests that digital technology is smart, is environmentally benign and adheres to a logic far removed from the industrial, extractivist, fossil-fuelled and polluting activity characteristic of twentieth-century industrial capitalism. The truth, however, could not be further from the fantasy of dematerialisation that accompanies digital technologies.

Focusing on 5G shifts our attention away from the consumption of thin client devices such as smartphones, towards the material and energy costs and spectacular levels of waste associated with the infrastructures that are required for thin client devices to function. This includes both internet infrastructure, such as hyperscale and cloud datacentres, fibre-optic cables, cable landing stations and internet exchange points; and 5G-specific infrastructure, such as small cell base stations, radio access network towers, multiple-input multiple-output antennae and distributed servers. These infrastructures are designed to be functionally invisible, to recede into the background of everyday life,[3] despite the fact that they enable the telecommunication that is central to our highly mediated existence.

Digital technologies, such as 5G-compatible devices and the infrastructure that enables those devices to operate, are immensely complex artefacts whose small size belies their material and energy costs.[4] For example, a smartphone typically weighs around 150 grams but requires approximately 75 kilograms of material to be extracted from the earth, and has a lifetime carbon footprint of 70–120 kilograms of CO_2e.[5] Of the waste associated with a smartphone, 99.9 per cent comes from producing the device, not from discarding it. Smartphones contain between 60 and 70 different elements[6] which are unevenly geologically distributed, causing dependency on particular reserves such as Congolese tantalum and cobalt, Chinese rare earth elements, Chilean lithium and copper, and so on.

The highly purified materials whose specific affordances are leveraged within high-performance computational assemblages bear little resemblance to the ores extracted from the ground. For example, the electrolytically refined copper used for interconnects within microprocessors and for wiring throughout microelectronics is over 99.99 per cent pure. This contrasts with the chalcopyrite ore extracted from mines, whose average purity declined over the twentieth century from 2 per cent to just 0.8 per cent as sources of high-grade copper ores were depleted.[7] This means that over 99 per cent of the extracted matter (which often comes from open-cast mines that deplete biodiversity) is waste. The processes used to purify materials such as copper – crushing and pulverising rock, froth flotation, smelting, and the final stage of electrolysis – all require immense amounts of energy and generate additional volumes of waste material, much of which is toxic. Soils in areas proximate to copper-mine tailings (the liquid waste produced during extraction) are contaminated with heavy metals including copper, iron, cobalt, lead, zinc and magnesium.[8] The waste produced by extracting materials for 5G and other digital technologies is not just aesthetically unappealing, it poisons lands predominantly located in the global periphery, while the profits from those technologies largely accumulate in the global core under the neocolonial process of ecologically unequal exchange.[9]

In addition to the wasteful and toxic processes associated with producing digital technologies and infrastructure for 5G, a lack of compatibility with previous 4G LTE infrastructure results in 5G inevitably becoming a significant driver of infrastructural waste and contributing to a wasteful upgrade culture predicated upon planned obsolescence. Indeed, one distinguishing feature of each named numerical shift in wireless cellular connectivity is the lack of backwards compatibility with previous generations. 5G operates on different spectrum frequencies from 4G LTE, with 5G including the capability to use millimetre wave spectrum (24+ GHz), enabling the use of higher bandwidths and lower latencies when compared to the lower-frequency waves used in 4G LTE. However, higher-frequency waves require smaller cells,[10] necessitating larger numbers of base stations, cell towers, masts, antennae and other equipment that are located closer to one another to prevent signal distortion. While millimetre-wave 5G facilitates more devices connecting at higher speeds, this requires substantially more materials and produces more waste than previous mobile cellular infrastructures.

The lack of compatibility with 4G LTE networks, which as of 2022 comprise the majority of globally existent mobile cellular networks, entails that for the foreseeable future 5G infrastructure will exist alongside 4G LTE infrastructure rather than replacing it.[11] Having multiple levels of incompatible infrastructure is deeply wasteful, as it requires mobile network providers to produce and install enough base stations, towers, antennae and other associated infrastructure to provide adequate spatial coverage and connection speeds for customers equipped with either 4G or 5G devices.

Furthermore, the lack of backwards compatibility means that eventually, users of older forms of mobile connectivity will come under pressure to upgrade to 5G-compatible devices, as mobile network providers transition away from 4G LTE infrastructure. This process, whereby network providers compel consumers to upgrade functional 'older' devices by withdrawing infrastructural support from them, is commonly encountered across digital technologies and forms one element of the heavily criticised phenomena of planned obsolescence.[12] Prematurely curtailing the useful life of materially and energetically costly artefacts in order to effectively force users into upgrading enhances corporate profits at the cost of generating unnecessary waste and consumption. It is important here to situate planned obsolescence within the context of the Capitalocene,[13] a time when multiple planetary ecological boundaries have been breached with calamitous consequences for people both today and in the future.[14] Many of the worst outcomes in terms of drought, floods, famine and displacement are and will continue to be experienced by populations who have done little to contribute to ecological crises that largely result from the spectacular levels of overproduction and overconsumption associated with a relatively small fraction of wealthy and privileged humans.

The devices and infrastructures rendered obsolete by shifting to 5G will also substantially add to the growing volume of electronic waste. In 2021, over 57 million tonnes of e-waste was discarded.[15] As with many twenty-first-century ecological crises, this veritable mountain of toxic waste is produced highly unequally, with wealthy countries in the global economic core, such as the USA, the UK and Australia, contributing over 40 times more e-waste per capita than some countries located in the global periphery.[16]

Despite the significant material and energy costs and the immense amount of waste associated with 5G, technology companies argue that 5G will assist in transitioning towards a sustainable, green economy, enabling reductions in energy consumption across numerous sectors. Their audacious claims that 5G will have enabled a 15 per cent reduction in global greenhouse gas emissions by the end of 2020 are empirically false.[17] These industry-sourced figures are corporate greenwash designed to mask the significant environmental impacts of 5G. Refuting these claims, independent analysis predicts that the total energy consumption of mobile network technology will rise 160 per cent between 2019 and 2030, from 19.8 to 51.3 million tons of oil equivalent, predominantly because of the introduction of 5G.[18]

One of the industry's central claims alleging environmental benefits of 5G is that the technology will be more energy-efficient than 4G LTE, with base stations able to enter a 'sleep mode' when no devices are actively connected to them. However, improving efficiency does not come close to reducing the overall environmental impact arising from a larger volume of networking equipment handling vastly more data than previous infrastructures. This exemplifies the kind of rebound effect associated with increasing efficiency in growth-based economies; while energy is used more efficiently, the overall usage of energy (and production of waste) rises, and ultimately it is aggregate usage and waste generation that matters when considering sustainability.[19]

The context of contemporary ecological crisis in the Capitalocene strongly suggests the need for digital technology to embrace the kind of democratically planned reductions in energy and material usage (and in production of waste) associated with emergent positions surrounding degrowth.[20] This does not equate to a homogenous reduction in digital technology or denying connectivity to those who currently lack access; it requires curtailing the processes of planned obsolescence and production of incompatible infrastructures, while focusing on how digital technologies can help to build sustainable and democratic futures, rather than maximising corporate profits at the cost of excessive waste, energy and material use.

5G has featured prominently in conspiracy theories proclaiming it responsible for the transmission of the COVID-19 virus, or part of a Bill

Gates-led plot to microchip and control humanity.[21] Not only are these sweeping claims entirely baseless, they obfuscate the far more mundane damage enacted by 5G. The waste and other environmental degradation associated with 5G do not represent a secretive, malevolent plot by evil elites: they are an integral part of the structural logic of twenty-first-century digital capitalism.

Notes

1. Bruce Sterling, 'The life and death of media', in *Sound Unbound: Sampling digital music and culture*, ed. by Paul D. Miller (MIT Press, 2008), pp. 73–82.
2. Sy Taffel, 'Data and oil: Metaphor, materiality and metabolic rifts', *New Media & Society*, June 2021, <https://doi.org/10.1177/14614448211017887> [accessed 30 October 2022].
3. Susan Leigh Star, 'The ethnography of infrastructure', *American Behavioral Scientist* 43:3 (1999), pp. 377–91, <https://doi.org/10.1177/00027649921955326> [accessed 30 October 2022]; Mark Weiser, 'The computer for the 21st century', *Scientific American* 265:3 (1991), pp. 94–104.
4. For details, see Lisa Parks & Nicole Starosielski, *Signal Traffic: Critical studies of media infrastructures* (University of Illinois Press, 2015); Jussi Parikka, *A Geology of Media* (University of Minnesota Press, 2015); Sean Cubitt, *Finite Media: Environmental implications of digital technologies* (Duke University Press, 2017); Kate Crawford, *The Atlas of AI: Power politics and the planetary costs of artificial intelligence* (Yale University Press, 2021).
5. Apple, 'iPhone 12 Pro Max product environmental report', 13 October 2020, <https://www.apple.com/environment/pdf/products/iphone/iPhone_12_Pro_Max_PER_Oct2020.pdf> [accessed 30 October 2022]; IEEE (Institute of Electrical and Electronics Engineers), 'IEEE experts identify the fourth R-word in sustainability: Repair', *Cision PR Newswire*, 22 April 2013, <https://www.prnewswire.com/news-releases/ieee-experts-identify-the-fourth-r-word-in-sustainability---repair-204082861.html> [accessed 8 January 2023].
6. Brian Rohrig, 'Smartphones', *ChemMatters* 12 (2015).
7. Rembrandt Koppelaar & Henk Koppelaar, 'The ore grade and depth influence on copper energy inputs', *BioPhysical Economics and Resource Quality* 1:2 (2016), article 11, <https://doi.org/10.1007/s41247-016-0012-x> [accessed 30 October 2022].
8. Leonce Dusengemungu, Benjamin Mubemba & Cousins Gwanama, 'Evaluation of heavy metal contamination in copper mine tailing soils of Kitwe and Mufulira, Zambia, for reclamation prospects', *Nature Scientific Reports* 12 (2022), article 11283, <https://doi.org/10.1038/s41598-022-15458-2> [accessed 30 October 2022].
9. Christian Dorninger, Alf Hornborg, David J. Abson, Henrik Von Wehrden, Anke Schaffartzik, Stefan Giljum, John-Oliver Engler et al., 'Global patterns of ecologically unequal exchange: Implications for sustainability in the 21st century', *Ecological Economics* 179 (2021), article 106824.
10. A cell base station, tower or site is a location where antennae and associated information and communications equipment are situated. The network of base stations forms the cellular network used by smartphones. While urban 4G cells tend to be around 1 km in radius, millimetre wave 5G reduces this distance to approximately 250 m. Amy Nordrum & Kristen Clark, 'Everything you need to know about 5G', *IEEE Spectrum*, 27 January 2017, <https://spectrum.ieee.org/everything-you-need-to-know-about-5g> [accessed 30 October 2022].
11. Significant volumes of mobile wireless connectivity, especially in the global periphery, still rely upon the older 3G and 2G infrastructures.
12. Joseph Guiltinan, 'Creative destruction and destructive creations: Environmental ethics and planned obsolescence', *Journal of Business Ethics* 89:1 (2009), pp. 19–28, <https://doi.org/10.1007/s10551-008-9907-9> [accessed 30 October 2022]; Sy Taffel, 'AirPods and the earth: Digital technologies, planned obsolescence and the Capitalocene', *Environment and Planning E: Nature and Space*, January 2022, <https://doi.org/10.1177/25148486221076136> [accessed 30 October 2022].

13   Jason W. Moore, *Capitalism in the Web of Life: Ecology and the accumulation of capital* (Verso Books, 2015).
14   As of 2022, five of the planetary boundaries identified by Rockström et al. have been identified as being overshot. These are climate change, genetic diversity (biodiversity), land system change, biogeochemical flows and novel entities (the anthropogenic production of materials such as plastics). See Johan Rockström, Will L. Steffen, Kevin Noone, Åsa Persson, F. Stuart Chapin III, Eric Lambin, Timothy M. Lenton et al., 'Planetary boundaries: Exploring the safe operating space for humanity', *Ecology and Society* 14:2 (2009), article 32, <https://www.ecologyandsociety.org/vol14/iss2/art32/> [accessed 28 December 2022].
15   Vanessa Forti, Cornelis P. Balde, Ruediger Kuehr & Garam Bel, *The Global E-Waste Monitor 2020: Quantities, flows and the circular economy potential* (United Nations University, 2020).
16   We should also note that significant inequalities in terms of digital access, digital consumption and the production of digital waste exist within different regions and individuals located in any given nation-state.
17   Huawei, 'Green 5G: Building a sustainable world', August 2020, <https://www-file.huawei.com/-/media/corp2020/pdf/public-policy/green_5g_building_a_sustainable_world_v1.pdf?la=en> [accessed 30 October 2022].
18   Lian Jye Su, *Environmentally Sustainable 5G Deployment: Energy consumption analysis and best practices* (ABI Research, 2020).
19   John Bellamy Foster, Brett Clark & Richard York, 'Capitalism and the curse of energy efficiency', *Monthly Review* 62:6 (2010), pp. 1–12.
20   For example, see Jason Hickel, *Less Is More: How degrowth will save the world* (Random House, 2020); Matthias Schmelzer, Andrea Vetter & Aaron Vansintjan, *The Future Is Degrowth: A guide to a world beyond capitalism* (Verso Books, 2022).
21   Jack Goodman & Flora Carmichael, 'Coronavirus: 5G and microchip conspiracies from around the world', BBC, 27 June 2020, <https://www.bbc.com/news/53191523> [accessed 30 October 2022].

7 dear things

Maja and Reuben Fowkes

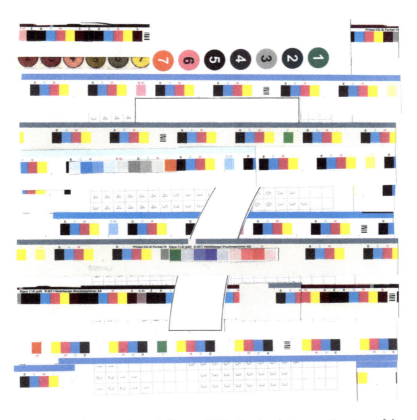

Figure 7.0 Nina Mathijsen, *Collage 7*, 2021. © takeadetour.eu. Courtesy of the artist.

The etymology of 'waste' leads back to a medieval usage that connotes the dystopian prospects of a world reshaped by climate change: a desolate uninhabited region. Wastelands are recognisable today in the sacrifice zones of extractive industry as devastated, uncared-for, denatured landscapes where life fails to flourish. Environmental historians Raj Patel and Jason W. Moore singled out nature, money, work, care, food, energy and lives as 'seven cheap things' that are vital to the development of the modern world.[1] Since the Late Middle Ages, these seven building blocks of modernity have been systematically cheapened within the capitalist economy in accordance with the market equation of reducing external costs to maximise profits. It is in making visible the chasm between the real value of the liveliness of nature, the creativity of work and the power of care and their paradoxical cheapness under capitalism that the prospects lie to restore the wastes of an exhausted and overheating planet.

The starting point of Patel and Moore's account is another moment of climate crisis, the period of global cooling known as the Little Ice Age that began in the fourteenth century, bringing crop failures which, compounded by the Black Death pandemic, saw the population of Europe shrink by more than a third. With the feudal social and economic order unravelling, and the supply of cheap work, money and food threatened, capitalism found a profitable solution in debt-fuelled warfare and colonialism. By reorienting the economy around the colonial frontier, the cheapness of human and non-human natures and their availability for exploitation was assured for centuries to come. Capitalism may have weathered the storm of the Little Ice Age and rebooted the strategy of seven cheap things through the pursuit of militarism and colonialism, but the planetary crisis of climate change poses a more fundamental challenge, threatening to turn the entire biosphere into a barren waste.

Despite the hopes invested in technological panaceas, the economics of the seven cheap things has come up against an immovable external limit in the form of escalating ecological breakdown. In the face of extreme weather and encroaching desertification, the bioengineered nature on monocultural farms is becoming uneconomic and unviable. Ageing populations, re-emerging barriers to transnational migration and the stirrings of a collective refusal of the exploitative conditions of industrial, agricultural and domestic labour are restricting the flow of cheap work. The stream of cheap fossil fuel energy is likewise tempered by the realisation that it would be suicidal to allow global temperatures to rise by more than two degrees. Near-zero interest rates and financial engineering have for now kept the cost of borrowing artificially low, deferring and delaying the unavoidable reckoning with the ecological consequences of capitalist growth. An alternative trajectory may still be possible, but this would depend on abandoning the profit-seeking paradigm of cheapness and embracing the seven dear things that make the difference between the flourishing of life in all its diversity and the wastes of a postapocalyptic future.

Note

1   Raj Patel & Jason W. Moore, *A History of the World in Seven Cheap Things: A guide to capitalism, nature, and the future of the planet* (Verso, 2018).

8: Octopus

Tina Beigi

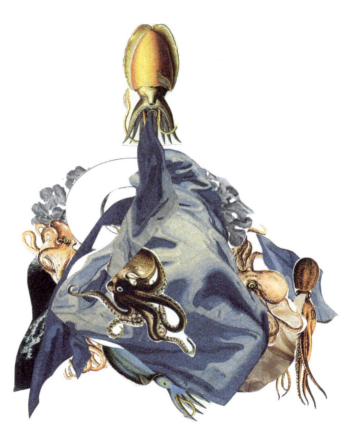

Figure 8.0 Nina Mathijsen, *Collage 8*, 2021. © takeadetour.eu. Courtesy of the artist.

The octopus is a scavenger: making good use of its eight tentacles, the cephalopod collects piles of broken scallop shells and converts them into shelters. Lately, favourite hiding spots have also included ceramic pots, metal pipes, rusted cans and beer bottles. This devious escape artist endowed with a large, complex nervous system is an incredibly intelligent problem-solver. In regions where human tourists collect an excessive number of seashells, the octopuses find alternatives in copious human garbage.

Upon close examination, the octopus's garden is a seabed junkyard. In 'Octopolis', a den of 'gloomy octopuses' (*Octopus tetricus*) off the coast of Jervis Bay in Australia, divers found a 12-inch-long piece of garbage from a boat, which had been neatly arranged to fit the seascape.[1] Assembling around the inescapable presence of human trash in the marine environment, octopuses have increasingly chosen manufactured remains instead of seashells or coral as dwellings. A newly discovered species, the pygmy octopus in Brazil (*Paroctopus cthulhu*), has only ever been observed sheltering in litter.[2] Even deep-sea octopuses in the Mediterranean are making use of sinking rubbish, which raises the question: is the octopus a natural-born circular economist, turning waste streams into wealth?

Camouflage and ink squirting are among the behaviours that allow octopuses to survive in the ocean. Owing to their soft body, these molluscs are unprotected when hunting their prey; a shell can therefore provide more safety and increase their chances of survival. However, these mineral shells are cumbersome to lug around. By contrast, plastic cups are lightweight and durable and have become the octopus's favourite exoskeleton.

Every so often, on the deep-sea highway, an upside-down plastic cup from which eight limbs creep out wanders past the shell-lives. Octopus fondness for plastic scaffolding may result from the added visual value that transparent plastic cups offer in addition to weightlessness. And yet, to the scientists' surprise, broken glass bottles are also used by octopuses as headcover, despite their heaviness: bottles once used as pharmaceutical product packaging find their way into the octopus's wardrobe. But such 'full metal jackets' do not come free of peril. Cadmium is a toxic chemical found in plastics, glass, batteries and many other common ocean pollutants. After exposure to cadmium, octopuses panic and synthesise a heat shock protein called Hsp70, which protects cells from the damaging effect of metabolic stress.[3]

Perhaps not unrelated to their metabolic stress, back in Octopolis, researchers also witnessed 'trash' behaviour: males and females alike exhibit vicious acts of aggression and eject one another from their synthetic dens.[4] Far from the garden of Eden, Octopolis represents the lapsarian fall on the seafloor.

Despite the risks attached to hazardous trash, the octopuses find many usages for such items. Instead of bottling up their emotions, female octopuses apply trash-throwing skills, usually during den building or housekeeping, against males when feeling harassed! If the male survives this spring-cleaning ritual, he may not survive the lovemaking. The female typically kills and eats her own means of reproduction once the male has fulfilled his function. She playfully hugs the male with three arms and strangles him to death before gobbling him up into the recycling bin of her belly, where he will nourish the babies in the making. The octopus never wastes: it scavenges and repurposes human debris and sexual partners alike. This circular economy keeps turning: after laying a clutch of eggs, the mother stops eating, and by the time the eggs hatch, she dies.[5] Octopuses are serious cannibals, and a biologically programmed ignominious end is perhaps their way to keep mothers from eating their young. Lab reports have even shown that captive females deliberately accelerate the death spiral, banging into the edges of the tank, pulling off chunks of skin, or chewing the tips of their own tentacles.[6] As a semelparous species, the octopus reproduces once before dying. By self-mutilating, the octopuses repurpose their abandoned bodies and provide food abundance to the newborn.

So, yes: the octopus is a natural-born circular economist, turning waste – marine and land-based alike – into wealth.

Notes

1 Peter Godfrey-Smith, David Scheel, Stephanie Chancellor, Stefan Linquist & Matthew Lawrence, 'In the line of fire: Debris throwing by wild octopuses', *PLoS ONE* 17:11 (2022), article e0276482 <https://doi.org/10.1371/journal.pone.0276482> [accessed 29 December 2022].
2 Tatiana S. Leite, Erica A. G. Vidal, Françoise D. Lima, Sergio M. Q. Lima, Ricardo M. Dias, Giulia A. Giuberti, Davi de Vasoncellos et al., 'A new species of pygmy *Paroctopus* Naef, 1923 (Cephalopoda: Octopodidae): the smallest southwestern Atlantic octopod, found in sea debris', *Marine Biodiversity* 51, article 68 (2021) <https://doi.org/10.1007/s12526-021-01201-z> [accessed 3 January 2023].
3 Ling-Li Long, Ying-Li Han, Zhang Sheng, Chen Du, You-Fa Wang & Jun-Quan Zhu, 'Expression analysis of HSP70 in the testis of *Octopus tankahkeei* under thermal stress', *Comparative Biochemistry and Physiology Part A: Molecular & Integrative Physiology* 187 (2015), pp. 150–9, <https://doi.org/10.1016/j.cbpa.2015.05.022> [accessed 3 January 2023].
4 David Scheel, Stephanie Chancellor, Martin Hing, Matthew Lawrence, Stefan Linquist & Peter Godfrey-Smith, 'A second site occupied by Octopus tetricus at high densities, with notes on their ecology and behavior', *Marine and Freshwater Behaviour and Physiology* 50:4 (2017), pp. 285–91.

5   Z. Yan Wang & Clifton W. Ragsdale, 'Multiple optic gland signaling pathways implicated in octopus maternal behaviors and death', *Journal of Experimental Biology* 221:19 (2018), jeb185751 <https://doi.org/10.1242/jeb.185751> [accessed 27 October 2022].
6   Z. Yan Wang, Melissa R. Pergande, Clifton W. Ragsdale & Stephanie M. Cologna, 'Steroid hormones of the octopus self-destruct system', *Current Biology* 32:11 (2022), pp. 2572–9.e4, <https://doi.org/10.1016/j.cub.2022.04.043> [accessed 3 January 2023].

9/11: Remains

Michael Hennessy Picard

Figure 9.0 Nina Mathijsen, *Collage 9*, 2021. © takeadetour.eu. Courtesy of the artist.

In the months after the 9/11 attack on the World Trade Center (WTC), which killed thousands of people and cost US$40 billion (£29 billion) in damages, the shock at the tower collapse gave way to the monstrous scale of the rescue and clean-up operation in New York.

Amid the destruction, an improvised team of volunteers, fire-fighters, police and detection dogs found 21 people alive on the first day, but none thereafter. The remaining body parts would be painstakingly collected in 21,900 pieces scattered throughout the skyscrapers' debris. This uneasy piece of forensic work would haunt the American psyche, with intriguing side-effects and aftershocks.

The authorities designated a Staten Island landfill as a site where the tower debris was transported to be sorted and inspected for human residues. Evocatively called 'Fresh Kills' (from the Middle Dutch word *kille*, meaning 'stream'), the suburban landfill had served since 1948 as the primary disposal facility for the solid waste of New York City (NYC). Over time, according to the then NYC mayor, Rudy Giuliani, it became 'the world's largest landfill'.

The landfill would soon become a site for the costliest forensic investigation in US history, involving DNA identification of damaged bone and statistical analysis of partial profiles. But, sifting through the melted computers, corroded steel, broken glass, ash and dust, analysts could not systematically identify and separate the human remains from architectural debris. Fresh Kills became a graveyard for unidentifiable bodies.

But the human remains generated by 9/11 were not fully contained at Fresh Kills. The Department of Design and Construction contracted five construction companies to clear the rubble of the WTC from Ground Zero (in order to reopen Wall Street as quickly as possible, the NYC Department of Sanitation deployed thousands of staff to clean the area around the Stock Exchange and lower Manhattan in general). Families of victims objected that the authorities improperly handled body remains. Piles of organic and non-organic waste from the rubble of the Twin Towers had, they argued, been hastily displaced and indistinctly buried along with conventional sources of municipal waste.

An affidavit filed in 2007 before a Manhattan Federal Court reveals that the remains, mixed with debris powders known as 'fines', had been allegedly carried away by city employees to fill ruts and potholes in NYC. The remains of a privately owned vertical tower had been used to patch a broken horizontal public road network. As the families of victims filed a lawsuit for mismanagement of human remains against the municipality, the authorities objected that the debris had been inspected following a meticulous process of classification. In the end, the judge sided with NYC. He said: 'the victims perished without leaving a trace, utterly consumed into incorporeality by the intense, raging fires, or pulverized into dust by the massive tons of collapsing concrete and steel'.[1]

But still the human remains spread. The monstrous ruins further escaped the attempt to control them, their toxic vapours proving harmful to the workers on site. In Manhattan, the death toll escalated, reaching the lives of construction workers, medics and others exposed to contaminants and likely to contract deadly illnesses after the attack. The rescue and reconstruction projects created new human remains. Thousands of tonnes of pulverised concrete, construction debris, cellulose, asbestos, lead and mercury, and fire dioxins increased the risk of kidney, heart, liver and breast cancer among first respondents. Over the next decade, surviving first responders filed workers' compensation claims and sued NYC for failing to provide proper protective equipment at Ground Zero, until the passing of the 9/11 Health and Compensation Act, a law created to provide them with medical care.

The non-human remains of 9/11 had a different fate. Though the site was considered a health hazard, the towers' structural steel was not. The scrap metal industry bought the buildings' remains and sold them for profit to Chinese and Indian second-hand metal markets. One scrap processor under contract with the NYC Department of Sanitation purchased and cut down the metal at Fresh Kills with torching equipment. Another company, Shanghai Baosteel Group, bought an additional 50,000 tonnes of large structural beams auctioned by NYC at US$120 (£87) a tonne.

Despite an early and unsuccessful attempt by Greenpeace to qualify the scrap exports as hazardous and ban their repurposing in the 'Global South', the steel reached India within six months of the tragedy. Several buildings were built with Twin Tower steel across Indian cities, including a college, a car maintenance yard, arcades and … a trade centre.

The story of 9/11 provides a stark example of the political economy of waste management, which profoundly shapes the culture of the modern metropolis. 'Waste' is not an undesired by-product of human society but contributes to the cycles of boom and bust. A regime of land reclamation has covered up the presence of 9/11's dead. As Wall Street reopened, Silverstein Properties and the Lower Manhattan Development Corporation oversaw the reconstruction of the site, including the erection of six new office towers, the highest one being One World Trade Center. Totemic symbols of wealth surround Ground Zero to ensure the institutional continuity of the financial corporation. Since 2008, the Fresh Kills dumping ground has gradually morphed into a municipal recreational park, accessible by bike, canoe and horseback. Once completed, the expansive area will be almost three times the size of Central Park and covered in vegetation and synthetic playgrounds. A marshland in the nineteenth century, Fresh Kills is now an eco-park, including a human-made wetland, secured by a system for the capture and treatment of underground toxic gases that heats 20,000 local homes.

This is not a new process. In July 2010, construction of the Ground Zero memorial ground to a halt when remains of an eighteenth-century ship were found in the mud. It was speculated that the hull of this wooden ship was used as part of the debris in a landfill to extend the island of Manhattan into the Hudson River. Historically, New York used the rubble of its construction operations and wreckage of its seaport to create artificial land and expand its waterfront. Much like other prized real estate still standing today, the Twin Towers were originally built on the site of a former landfill in Lower Manhattan, following a law of ruins according to which 'capital is built upon the foundations of its own refuse'.[2]

Notes

1 WTC Families for a Proper Burial, Inc. v. City of New York, 567 F.Supp.2d 529, 531–32 (S.D.N.Y., 2008).
2 Jani Scandura, *Down in the Dumps: Place, Modernity, American Depression* (Duke University Press, 2008), p. 3.

Epilogue

Tamar Garb

The invitation to write an epilogue for this wonderful *Wastiary* allows me to make good on an experience that might well have gone to waste. Could this exercise, I wonder, like writing itself, operate as a kind of salvage operation designed to conserve and process experience that might otherwise be left to rot or wither away?

After a six-month sojourn amongst the variant-vilified and the 'shunned', the hapless inhabitants of 'COVID-19 red-listed' countries placed at the mercy of politicians, bureaucrats and profiteers, I found myself, in June 2021, marooned in a quarantine hotel in Hayes, west London, trying to make use of my time. I was unable even to exercise in the lowly car park (Figure ZZ.1), covered in bird excrement and suffused with traffic fumes, where numbed quarantiners were allowed to circulate, zombie-like, under the bored eyes of the zero-hours, minimum-wage guards, for their allocated 10-minute slots. Instead, I was stuck indoors and measured out my days in Nescafé sachets and long-life milk, sipped from disposable cups. The denial of the daily somnambulists' trudge came like a bolt on my mobile when NHS 'track and trace' informed me that my isolation in the Marriott Hotel was not enough and that, having been in contact with an infected person (presumably on the plane), I was now unable to leave my room. This was on day three of an 11-day sojourn in an air-conditioned box *sans* fresh air or sunshine or space to stretch one's legs. I feared I would waste away. Time had to be spent within the confines of a room designed to be occupied for a night.

The carceral experience was bizarre and unreal. It was certainly neither healthy nor 'safe'. Besides the enforced sedentary regime (punctuated periodically by online Pilates or pacing the floor in small circles), the day was structured round the regular delivery of meals,

Figure ZZ.1 *Car park at the quarantine hotel*. Photograph by Tamar Garb, June 2021. Courtesy of the author.

left in brown paper bags at the door. Ordered on day one for the entire stay, it was impossible to know what would arrive at each mealtime. What was certain, though, was that much of it would be inedible (oily, over-salted and starchy, with little choice beyond different versions of ersatz 'Indian' stodge), so it was destined to be chucked out along with the copious non-biodegradable packaging in which it was unceremoniously placed (Figure ZZ.2). Water was delivered regularly in 500-millilitre plastic bottles so that it accumulated like a conceptual artwork on the mantelpiece. I spaced each bottle carefully under the outsized flat-screen telly on which Freeview could be readily screened, measuring out the passing of time in the toxic accumulation of junk (Figure ZZ.3). Bags of crisps, plastic-wrapped cakes, boxed juices and condiments in small packages – mayonnaise, ketchup, salt and pepper – arrived thrice daily, and these mounted up in a neat pile, preserved in the hope that they could be taken home by the staff. But with fear of contamination and the end-of-stay sanitisation regime, they were bound, I suspect, to be binned. Hot dinners came packed in plastic cartons or silver foil wrappers, accompanied with disposable cutlery and synthetic tumblers. The garbage accumulated and was required to be packed in black bin bags and left for collection at the door. There it sat in the littered corridor policed by the

Figure ZZ.2 *Food at the quarantine hotel.* Photograph by Tamar Garb, June 2021. Courtesy of the author.

alienated guards and collected once a day to be disposed of in a giant waste truck situated in the forbidden exercise yard/car park.

The experience left me wondering about the cost of the whole endeavour. Not only the £1,750.00 I coughed up to be detained at Her Majesty's pleasure, or the weight on the public purse, but also the toll that this system will take on our lives and our planet for decades. I appreciated the need for vigilance with Covid. I understood the motivation to police the borders and contain the import of variants. But there was much in the management of risk during the pandemic that made little sense to me and seemed criminally wasteful and callous. The whole infrastructure of hotel quarantine was supported by gig-economy labour. For one thing, the excess number of G4S guards made one smell a rat. They sat, poor things, garbed in yellow polyester high-vis vests in the passages, the lobbies, the lifts and landings, with their lists and tick-sheets and charts, pretending to clock one in and out of a room, or monitoring the exercise quad and the stairwells for delinquents and deviants, while all the while staring into their mobile phones and laps. The boredom was palpable. Being surveilled by these uniformed men recalled being in the Soviet Union in the 1980s, where ancient women sat by samovars

Figure ZZ.3 *Accumulated water bottles at the quarantine hotel.* Photograph by Tamar Garb, June 2021. Courtesy of the author.

in hotel corridors, ostensibly making tea but in fact keeping watch on the comings and goings of guests. There was little motivation for the government to end hotel quarantine given the hundreds of low-skilled workers it employed, and the rescue operation for the airport-based tourist industry that it sustained. Once quarantine was over, thousands of casual workers were back at the job centres looking to be recycled and placed. Like the plastic and unsorted muck that emerged from the hotels each day, along with the contaminated disposable masks and gloves, they needed to find a place on this Earth. But where the detritus and disinfectants are destined, fatally, to clog up the waterways and air, probably killing and polluting in greater numbers than the purported lives that they saved, who has calculated the wasted hours and potential that such alienated labour represents?

Most galling about the whole system of quarantine was the geopolitics that subtended its flawed but predictable logic. Experiencing much of the COVID-19 pandemic from South Africa, 'home' of variant Beta, I was acutely aware of how divisive and racially inflected the discourse on variants was. With all of southern Africa red-listed, even while travel from South Asia continued and was gradually being reopened (for example in German entry requirements), it was hard not to feel that one had been relegated to a 'shit-hole' country, whose citizens no-one in Europe would miss. Looking at the numbers of infections bore this out. At the time of my detention in June 2021, there were only nine new cases of the Beta variant in the UK (there were 54,268 of the Delta variant). Total cases as of 7 July 2021 amounted to 275,913 of the Alpha variant, 216,249 of the Delta and only 1,073 of the Beta. But there was no talk of letting vaccinated travellers from southern Africa gain entry to the UK. It was as if they were contaminated, not only by the virus (whether by the Beta or the increasingly ubiquitous Delta variant), but also by an indelible racialised stain that made them forever carriers of disease and infection. Why was it any more dangerous for a Pfizer-injected traveller, in possession of a negative PCR test, to enter from Namibia or Botswana, than from the USA or Canada or Greece? Granted, infections in South Africa were high. But they were not as high as in the UK, and the faltering vaccination roll-out was as much a problem of supply and patents and price as it was of failed infrastructure, corruption, ignorance and crippling bureaucracy.

So it's worth saying what everyone knows. That COVID-19 has not so much changed our perception of the world as shone a light on that which we already knew: that radical inequality leads to the wasting of lives, calculable now in numbers, of dead, of sick and of suffering; that short-term profits and proceeds invariably trump far-off, intangible goals that can appear like pipe-dreams in the mist; and that, despite the overwhelming odds stacked against salvage and sustainable life, there are acts of kindness and reflection and disinterest that fly in the face of entropy. This volume is one such instance, for, edited and designed under lockdown, it has managed to transform that which could be relegated to the bin into a treasure-trove of speculation and creative endeavour. Even the horrors of hotel quarantine can make one sit back and reflect.

Bibliography

Adams, David, Christopher De Sousa & Steven Tiesdell, 'Brownfield development: A comparison of North American and British approaches', *Urban Studies* 47 (2010), pp. 75–104.
AFP, 'French baby boy banned from having name containing tilde', *The Guardian*, 13 September 2017, <https://www.theguardian.com/lifeandstyle/2017/sep/13/french-baby-boy-banned-from-getting-name-containing-symbol> [accessed 15 June 2021].
Agard-Jones, Vanessa, 'Bodies in the system', *Small Axe*, 17 (2013), pp. 182–92.
Allen, Alistair, 'Containment landfills: The myth of sustainability', *Engineering Geology* 60 (2001), pp. 3–19.
Allen, Barry, 'The ethical artifact', in *Trash*, ed. by John Knechtel (MIT Press, 2007), pp. 198–213.
Amazon Sustainability – US, 'Our carbon footprint', <https://sustainability.aboutamazon.com/environment/carbon-footprint> [accessed 26 October 2022].
Appadurai, Arjun, 'Deep democracy: Urban governmentality and the horizon of politics', *Environment and Urbanisation* 13 (2001), pp. 23–44.
Apple, 'iPhone 12 Pro Max product environmental report', 13 October 2020, <https://www.apple.com/environment/pdf/products/iphone/iPhone_12_Pro_Max_PER_Oct2020.pdf> [accessed 30 October 2022].
Aronson, Jay, *Who Owns the Dead?* (Harvard University Press, 2017).
Balayannis, Angeliki, 'Routine exposures: Reimaging the visual politics of hazardous sites', *GeoHumanities* 5 (2019), pp. 572–90.
Balayannis, Angeliki, 'Toxic sights: The spectacle of hazardous waste removal', *Environment and Planning D: Society & Space* 38 (2020), pp. 772–90.
Balayannis, Angeliki & Emma Garnett, 'Chemical kinship: Interdisciplinary experiments with pollution', *Catalyst: Feminism, Theory, Technoscience* 6 (2020), pp. 1–10.
Bardmann, Theodor M., 'Wenn aus Arbeit Abfall wird – Überlegungen zur Umorientierung der industriesoziogischen Sichtweise', *Zeitschrift für Soziologie* 19 (1990), pp. 179–94.
Barlow, John Perry, 'A declaration of the independence of cyberspace', *Duke Law & Technology Review* 18:1 (2019), pp. 5–7.
Barr, Stewart et al., 'Beyond recycling: An integrated approach for understanding municipal waste management', *Applied Geography* 39 (2013), pp. 67–77.
Barry, Andrew, 'Pharmaceutical matters: The invention of informed materials', *Theory, Culture & Society* 22 (2005), pp. 51–69.
Barsalou, Olivier & Michael Hennessy Picard, 'International environmental law in an era of globalized waste', *Chinese Journal of International Law* 17:3 (2018), pp. 887–906.
Bastin, Jean-Francois et al., 'The global tree restoration potential', *Science* 365 (2019), pp. 76–9.
Baudrillard, Jean, *The Consumer Society: Myths and structures* (Sage, 1998).
Baudrillard, Jean, *The Illusion of the End* (Polity Press, 1994).
Bauman, Zygmunt, *Wasted Lives: Modernity and its outcasts* (Polity, 2003).
Beckett, Caitlynn, 'Beyond remediation: Containing, confronting and caring for the Giant Mine Monster', *Environment and Planning E: Nature and Space* 4:4 (2021), pp. 1389–412.

Beckett, Samuel, *Endgame* (Faber, 1958).
Bell, Lucy, 'Place, people and processes in waste theory: A Global South critique', *Cultural Studies* 33:1 (2019), pp. 98–121.
Bell, Lucy, Alex Flynn & Patrick O'Hare, *Taking Form, Making Worlds: Cartonera publishers in Latin America* (University of Texas Press, 2022).
Bellamy Foster, John, Brett Clark & Richard York, 'Capitalism and the curse of energy efficiency', *Monthly Review* 62:6 (2010), pp. 1–12.
Benkler, Yochai, 'From consumers to users: Shifting the deeper structures of regulation toward sustainable commons and user access', *Federal Communications Law Journal* 52 (1999), p. 561.
Bennett, Jane, *Vibrant Matter: A political ecology of things* (Duke University Press, 2010).
Bennett, Luke, 'The Bunker: Metaphor, materiality and management', *Culture & Organization* 17 (2011), pp. 155–73.
Benyera, Everisto (ed.), *Africa and the Fourth Industrial Revolution: Curse or cure?* (Springer, 2022).
Benyera, Everisto, *The Fourth Industrial Revolution and the Recolonisation of Africa: The coloniality of data* (Routledge, 2021).
Bettilyon, Tyler Elliot, 'How data hoarding is the new threat to privacy and climate change', *Medium*, 1 August 2019 <https://onezero.medium.com/how-data-hoarding-is-the-new-threat-to-privacy-and-climate-change-1e5a21a49494> [accessed 26 October 2022].
Bianchini, Ron, 'Are data centers the new global landfill?', *Wired*, October 2012 <https://www.wired.com/insights/2012/10/data-centers-new-global-landfill/> [accessed 26 October 2022].
Bond, William J. et al., 'The trouble with trees: Afforestation plans for Africa', *Trends in Ecology & Evolution* 34 (2019), pp. 963–5.
Borges, Jorge Luis, *The Aleph: Including the prose fictions from The Maker* (Penguin, 2000).
Bourdieu, Pierre & Loïc Wacquant, *An Invitation to Reflexive Sociology* (University of Chicago Press, 1992).
Brun, Cathryn, 'Active waiting and changing hopes: Toward a time perspective on protracted displacement', *Social Analysis* 59 (2015), pp. 19–37.
Bryant, Levi, 'Flat ontology', 24 February 2010, <https://larvalsubjects.wordpress.com/2010/02/24/flat-ontology-2/> [accessed 20 January 2022].
Cabaniss, Deborah L., 'Inside "Inside Out"', *The Lancet Psychiatry* 2 (2015), p. 789.
Chen, Mel Y., *Animacies: Biopolitics, racial mattering, and queer affect* (Duke University Press, 2012).
Chen, Mel Y., 'Toxic animacies, inanimate affections', *GLQ: A Journal of Lesbian and Gay Studies* 17:2–3 (2011), pp. 265–86.
Chrétien de Troyes, *The Complete Story of the Grail: Chrétien de Troyes' Perceval and its continuations*, trans. by Nigel Bryant (D. S. Brewer, 2015).
Citizens United v. Federal Election Commission, 558 U.S. 310 (2010) <https://www.supremecourt.gov/opinions/boundvolumes/558bv.pdf> [in the pdf, see p. 310 of the Reporter; accessed 30 December 2022].
Cohen, Jon, 'Meet the scientist painter who turns deadly viruses into beautiful works of art', *Science*, 11 April 2019, <https://www.sciencemag.org/news/2019/04/meet-scientist-painter-who-turns-deadly-viruses-beautiful-works-art> [accessed 3 April 2021].
Cohen, Julie E., *Between Truth and Power* (Oxford University Press, 2019).
Crawford, Kate, *The Atlas of AI: Power politics and the planetary costs of artificial intelligence* (Yale University Press, 2021).
Credit Suisse, *Global Wealth Report*, <https://www.credit-suisse.com/about-us/en/reports-research/global-wealth-report.html> [accessed 20 January 2022].
Crewe, Louise, 'Life itemised: Lists, loss, unexpected significance, and the enduring geographies of discard', *Environment and Planning D: Society and Space* 29 (2011), pp. 27–46.
Cubitt, Sean, *Finite Media: Environmental implications of digital technologies* (Duke University Press, 2017).
Darling, Jonathan, 'Forced migration and the city: Irregularity, informality, and the politics of presence', *Progress in Human Geography* 41:2 (2016), pp. 178–98.
De Broin, Michel, *Molysmocène*, Video projection on the façade of Théâtre Maisonneuve, Montreal, 2015.
de-Graft Aikins, Ama & Bernard Akoi-Jackson, '"Colonial virus": COVID-19, creative arts and public health communication in Ghana', *Ghana Medical Journal* 54:4 Supplement (2020), pp. 86–96 <https://doi.org/10.4314/gmj.v54i4s.13>.

de la Cadena, Marisol & Mario Blaser, eds., *A World of Many Worlds* (Duke University Press, 2018).

Department for Transport, *Integrated Rail Plan for the North and Midlands* (UK Government, November 2021), <https://assets.publishing.service.gov.uk/government/uploads/system/uploads/attachment_data/file/1062157/integrated-rail-plan-for-the-north-and-midlands-web-version.pdf> [accessed 30 October 2022].

Derrida, Jacques, *Archive Fever*, trans. by Eric Prenowitz (University of Chicago Press, 1995).

Dobbe, Roel & Meredith Whittaker, AI Now Institute, 'AI and climate change: How they're connected, and what we can do about it', *Medium*, 17 October, 2019, <https://medium.com/@AINowInstitute/ai-and-climate-change-how-theyre-connected-and-what-we-can-do-about-it-6aa8d0f5b32c> [accessed 26 October 2022].

Dorninger, Christian, Alf Hornborg, David J. Abson, Henrik Von Wehrden, Anke Schaffartzik, Stefan Giljum, John-Oliver Engler et al., 'Global patterns of ecologically unequal exchange: Implications for sustainability in the 21st century', *Ecological Economics* 179 (2021), article 106824.

Douglas, Mary, *Purity and Danger: An analysis of concepts of pollution and taboo* (Praeger, 1966).

Durkin, Joanne, Debra Jackson & Kim Usher, 'Touch in times of COVID-19: Touch hunger hurts', *Journal of Clinical Nursing* 30:1-2 (2021), pp. e4–e5, <https://doi.org/10.1111/jocn.15488>.

Dusengemungu, Leonce, Benjamin Mubemba & Cousins Gwanama, 'Evaluation of heavy metal contamination in copper mine tailing soils of Kitwe and Mufulira, Zambia, for reclamation prospects', *Nature Scientific Reports* 12 (2022), article 11283, <https://doi.org/10.1038/s41598-022-15458-2> [accessed 30 October 2022].

Efoui-Hess, Maxime, 'Climate crisis: The unsustainable use of online video', The Shift Project, 11 July 2019 <https://theshiftproject.org/wp-content/uploads/2019/07/2019-02.pdf> [accessed 26 October 2022].

Ehrenstein, Vera, 'Carbon sink geopolitics', *Economy and Society* 47 (2018), pp. 162–86.

Escobar, Arturo, *Designs for the Pluriverse: Radical interdependence, autonomy, and the making of worlds* (Duke University Press, 2018).

Farris Thompson, Robert, 'The aesthetics of the cool', *African Arts* 7:1 (1973), pp. 40–91.

Ferm, Jessica & Edward Jones, 'Beyond the post-industrial city: Valuing and planning for industry in London', *Urban Studies* 54 (2017), pp. 3380–98.

Field, T., 'American adolescents touch each other less and are more aggressive toward their peers as compared with French adolescents', *Adolescence* 34:136 (1999), pp. 753–8.

Forti, Vanessa, Cornelis P. Balde, Ruediger Kuehr & Garam Bel, *The Global E-Waste Monitor 2020: Quantities, flows and the circular economy potential* (United Nations University, 2020).

Freire Trigo, Sonia, *Vacant Land in London: Narratives of people, space, and time* (unpublished doctoral thesis, UCL, 2019).

Freire Trigo, Sonia, 'Vacant land in London: A planning tool to create land for growth', *International Planning Studies* 25 (2020), pp. 261–76.

Freud, Sigmund, *Civilisation and its Discontents* (Penguin Books, 2004 [1930]).

Freud, Sigmund, 'The Uncanny' [1919], in *The Standard Edition of the Complete Psychological Works of Sigmund Freud, XVII (1917–1919): An Infantile Neurosis and Other Works*, ed. by James Strachey and Anna Freud (The Hogarth Press and the Institute of Psychoanalysis, 1955), pp. 217–52.

George, Amber E., 'Reimagining human and nonhuman cohabitation', *Journal for Critical Animal Studies* 15:3 (2018), pp. 1–3.

Geraghty, Niall & Adriana Laura Massidda, 'The spatiality of desire in Martin Oesterheld's La Multitud and Luis Ortega's Dromómanos', in *Creative Spaces: Urban culture and marginality in Latin America*, ed. by Niall Geraghty and Adriana Laura Massidda (Institute of Latin American Studies, 2019), pp. 201–39.

Gille, Zsuzsa & Josh Lepawsky, eds, *The Routledge Handbook of Waste Studies* (Routledge, 2021).

Godfrey-Smith, Peter, David Scheel, Stephanie Chancellor, Stefan Linquist & Matthew Lawrence, 'In the line of fire: Debris throwing by wild octopuses', *PLoS ONE* 17:11 (2022), article e0276482 <https://doi.org/10.1371/journal.pone.0276482> [accessed 29 December 2022].

Goldstein, Jenny E., 'The afterlives of degraded tropical forests: New value for conservation and development', *Environment and Society* 5 (2014), pp. 124–40.

Goodman, Jack & Flora Carmichael, 'Coronavirus: 5G and microchip conspiracies from around the world', BBC, 27 June 2020, <https://www.bbc.com/news/53191523> [accessed 30 October 2022].

Gordillo, Gastón, *Rubble: The afterlife of destruction* (Duke University Press, 2014).

Graeber, David, 'Consumption', *Current Anthropology* 52 (2011), pp. 489–511.

Gregson, Nicky, Alan Metcalfe & Louise Crewe, 'Identity, mobility, and the throwaway society', *Environment and Planning D: Society and Space* 25 (2007), pp. 682–700.

Guiltinan, Joseph, 'Creative destruction and destructive creations: Environmental ethics and planned obsolescence', *Journal of Business Ethics* 89:1 (2009), pp. 19–28, <https://doi.org/10.1007/s10551-008-9907-9> [accessed 30 October 2022].

Hale, Thomas, *A Compleat Body of Husbandry* [...], Vol. I, 2nd ed. (London, 1758).

Hao, Karen, 'Training a single AI model can emit as much carbon as five cars in their lifetimes', *MIT Technology Review*, 6 June 2019, <https://www.technologyreview.com/s/613630/training-a-single-ai-model-can-emit-as-much-carbon-as-five-cars-in-their-lifetimes/> [accessed 26 October 2022].

Haraway, Donna, *Staying with the Trouble: Making kin in the Chthulucene* (Duke University Press, 2016).

Hawkins, Gay, *The Ethics of Waste* (Rowman & Littlefield, 2006).

Hetherington, Kevin, 'Secondhandedness: Consumption, disposal, and absent presence', *Environment and Planning D: Society and Space* 22 (2004), pp. 157–73.

Hickel, Jason, *Less Is More: How degrowth will save the world* (Random House, 2020).

High Speed One, <https://highspeed1.co.uk/> [accessed 30 October 2022].

High Speed Two, <https://www.hs2.org.uk/> [accessed 30 October 2022].

High Speed Two, *HS2: Realising the potential* (UK Government, 2018), <https://assets.hs2.org.uk/wp-content/uploads/2018/07/17154802/22403_Realising_the_potential_WEB.pdf> [accessed 30 October 2022].

Hogan, Mél, 'Data flows and water woes: The Utah Data Center', *Big Data & Society* 2:2 (2015), p. 1.

Horkheimer, Max & Theodor W. Adorno, *Dialectics of Enlightenment* (Stanford University Press, 2002).

HS2 Rebellion, <https://www.hs2rebellion.earth/> [accessed 30 October 2022].

Huawei, 'Green 5G: Building a sustainable world, August 2020', <https://www-file.huawei.com/-/media/corp2020/pdf/public-policy/green_5g_building_a_sustainable_world_v1.pdf?la=en> [accessed 30 October 2022].

Hubau, Wannes et al., 'Asynchronous carbon sink saturation in African and Amazonian tropical forests', *Nature* 579 (2020), pp. 80–7.

Huyssen, Andreas, *Twilight Memories: Marking time in a culture of amnesia* (Routledge, 1995).

IEEE (Institute of Electrical and Electronics Engineers), 'IEEE experts identify the fourth R-word in sustainability: Repair', *Cision PR Newswire*, 22 April 2013, <https://www.prnewswire.com/news-releases/ieee-experts-identify-the-fourth-r-word-in-sustainability---repair-204082861.html> [accessed 8 January 2023].

Ingold, Tim, *The Perception of the Environment: Essays on livelihood, dwelling and skill* (Routledge, 2000).

Irwin, Aisling, 'The everything mapper', *Nature* 573 (2019), pp. 478–81.

Jasanoff, Sheila, 'Making order: Law and science in action', in *The Handbook of Science and Technology Studies*, ed. by Edward J. Hackett, Michael Lynch & Judy Wajcman (MIT Press, 2008), pp. 761–86.

Jasanoff, Sheila, ed., *States of Knowledge* (Taylor & Francis, 2004).

Jeevendrampillai, David, 'The making of a suburb', in *London's Urban Landscape: Another way of telling*, ed. by Christopher Tilley (UCL Press, 2019), pp. 178–203.

Judt, Tony, *Postwar: A history of Europe since 1945* (Random House, 2011).

Jung, Carl, 'Mind and Earth', in *The Collected Works of C.G. Jung, Volume 10: Civilization in Transition*, ed. by Herbert Read et al. (Routledge and Kegan Paul, 1964 [1927]), pp. 45–69.

Kale, Sirin, 'Skin hunger helps explain your desperate longing for human touch', *Wired UK*, 29 April 2020, <https://www.wired.co.uk/article/skin-hunger-coronavirus-human-touch> [accessed 28 September 2020].

Kennedy, Duncan, 'The stakes of law, or Hale and Foucault', *Legal Studies Forum* 15 (1991), p. 327.

Kennedy, Greg, *An Ontology of Trash: The disposable and its problematic nature* (SUNY Press, 2007).

Khan, Lina, 'Amazon's antitrust paradox', *Yale Law Journal* 126 (2017), pp. 710–805.

Koppelaar, Rembrandt & Henk Koppelaar, 'The ore grade and depth influence on copper energy inputs', *BioPhysical Economics and Resource Quality* 1:2 (2016), article 11, <https://doi.org/10.1007/s41247-016-0012-x> [accessed 30 October 2022].

Leite, Tatiana S., Erica A. G. Vidal, Françoise D. Lima, Sergio M. Q. Lima, Ricardo M. Dias, Giulia A. Giuberti, Davi de Vasoncellos et al., 'A new species of pygmy *Paroctopus* Naef, 1923 (Cephalopoda: Octopodidae): The smallest southwestern Atlantic octopod, found in sea debris', *Marine Biodiversity* 51, article 68 (2021), <https://doi.org/10.1007/s12526-021-01201-z> [accessed 3 January 2023].

Lewis, Patrick John & Katia Hildebrandt, *Storytelling as Qualitative Research* (SAGE Publications Limited, 2020).

Liboiron, Max & Josh Lepawsky, *Discard Studies: Wasting, systems, and power* (MIT Press, 2022).

Liboiron, Max, Manuel Tironi & Nerea Calvillo, 'Toxic politics: Acting in a permanently polluted world', *Social Studies of Science* 48 (2018), pp. 331–49.

Long, Ling-Li, Ying-Li Han, Zhang Sheng, Chen Du, You-Fa Wang & Jun-Quan Zhu, 'Expression analysis of HSP70 in the testis of *Octopus tankahkeei* under thermal stress', *Comparative Biochemistry and Physiology Part A: Molecular & Integrative Physiology* 187 (2015), pp. 150–9, <https://doi.org/10.1016/j.cbpa.2015.05.022> [accessed 3 January 2023].

Lovejoy, Thomas E. & Carlos Nobre, 'Amazon tipping point', *Science Advances* 4 (2018).

Mahugija, John Andrew Marco, Bernhard Henkelmann & Karl-Werner Schramm, 'Levels and patterns of organochlorine pesticides and their degradation products in rainwater in Kibaha Coast Region, Tanzania', *Chemosphere* 118 (2015), pp. 12–19.

Marquardt, Franca, 'The Zapatistas' "Journey for Life" and its implications for a global solidarity', *Convivial Thinking*, 2 December 2021, <https://convivialthinking.org/index.php/2021/12/02/the-zapatistas-journey-for-life/> [accessed 11 November 2022].

McCabe, David & Karen Weise, 'Bezos and Zuckerberg take their pitches to Washington', *New York Times*, 19 September 2019, <https://www.nytimes.com/2019/09/19/business/bezos-zuckerberg-washington.html> [accessed 26 October 2022].

Melosi, Martin, *Fresh Kills: A history of consuming and discarding in New York City* (Columbia University Press, 2020).

Merchant, Brian, 'Amazon is aggressively pursuing big oil as it stalls out on clean energy', *Gizmodo*, 8 April 2019, <https://gizmodo.com/amazon-is-aggressively-pursuing-big-oil-as-it-stalls-ou-1833875828> [accessed 26 October 2022].

Meunier, Jacob, *On the Fast Track: French railway modernization and the origins of the TGV 1944–1983* (Praeger, 2002).

Miller School of Medicine, *Touch Research Institute (Archives)*, <https://med.miami.edu/centers-,-a-,-institutes/mailman-center/community/other-community-based-programs/touch-research-institute-(archives)> [accessed 30 December 2022].

Moore, Jason W., *Capitalism in the Web of Life: Ecology and the accumulation of capital* (Verso Books, 2015).

Moore, Jason, 'The Capitalocene Part I: On the nature and origins of our ecological crisis', *The Journal of Peasant Studies* 44:3 (2017), 595.

Morton, Timothy, *Hyperobjects: Philosophy and ecology after the end of the world* (University of Minnesota Press, 2013).

Mujila, Fiston Mwanza, *Tram 83* (Deep Vellum Publishing, 2016).

La multitud, dir. by Martin Oesterheld (J. C. Fisner, 2013).

Munteán, László, 'The remains of the day: The afterlife of the ruins of the World Trade Center', in *Places and Spaces of Monstrosity*, ed. by Rosalea Monacella (Inter-Disciplinary Press, 2014), pp. 69–78.

Murphy, Scott, 'HS2: Cheshire MP calls on government to scrap "white elephant"', *Northwich & Winsford Guardian*, 11 June 2022, <https://www.northwichguardian.co.uk/news/20201354.hs2-tatton-mp-calls-government-scrap-white-elephant/> [accessed 30 October 2022].

Nagy, Kelsi & Phillip David Johnson II, *Trash Animals: How we live with nature's filthy, feral, invasive, and unwanted species* (University of Minnesota Press, 2013).

NameMC, 'Coronavirus minecraft skins', <https://namemc.com/minecraft-skins/tag/coronavirus> [accessed 3 April 2021].

Natura Urbana: The Brachen of Berlin, dir. by Matthew Gandy (UK/Germany, 2017).

Negarestani, Reza, *Cyclonopedia: Complicity with anonymous materials* (re-press, 2008).

'The New Europeans: How waves of immigrants are reshaping a continent', *National Geographic*, October 2016, pp. 83–115.

Nordrum, Amy & Kristen Clark, 'Everything you need to know about 5G', *IEEE Spectrum*, 27 January 2017, <https://spectrum.ieee.org/everything-you-need-to-know-about-5g> [accessed 30 October 2022].

Oxfam International, 'Carbon emissions of richest 1 percent more than double the emissions of the poorest half of humanity', 21 September 2020, <https://www.oxfam.org/en/press-releases/carbon-emissions-richest-1-percent-more-double-emissions-poorest-half-humanity> [accessed 20 January 2022].

Parikka, Jussi, *A Geology of Media* (University of Minnesota Press, 2015).

Parks, Lisa & Nicole Starosielski, *Signal Traffic: Critical studies of media infrastructures* (University of Illinois Press, 2015).

Patel, Raj & Jason W. Moore, *A History of the World in Seven Cheap Things: A guide to capitalism, nature, and the future of the planet* (Verso, 2018).

Pellow, David Naguib, *Resisting Global Toxics: Transnational movements for environmental justice* (MIT Press, 2007).

Philippopoulos-Mihalopoulos, Andreas, *Spatial Justice: Body lawscape atmosphere* (Routledge, 2015).

Philippopoulos-Mihalopoulos, Andreas, 'We are all complicit: Performing law and water', in *Laws of the Sea*, ed. by Irus Braverman (Routledge, 2022), pp. 282–93.

Pietzsch, Natália et al., 'Benefits, challenges and critical factors of success for Zero Waste: A systematic literature review', *Waste Management* 67 (2017), pp. 324–53.

Pistor, Katharina, *The Code of Capital* (Princeton University Press, 2019).

Pratt, Laura A., 'Decreasing dirty dumping? A re-evaluation of toxic waste colonialism and the global management of transboundary hazardous waste', *William & Mary Environmental Law and Policy Review* 35 (2011), 582–623.

Privacy International, 'Buying a smart phone on the cheap? Privacy might be the price you have to pay', 20 September 2019, <https://privacyinternational.org/long-read/3226/buying-smart-phone-cheap-privacy-might-be-price-you-have-pay> [accessed 26 October 2022].

Ramakrishnan, Kavita & Tatiana A. Thieme, 'Peripheral humanitarianism: Ephemerality, experimentation, and effects of refugee provisioning in Paris', *Environment and Planning D: Society and Space* 40:5 (2022), pp. 763–85.

Randall, Vicky, 'Using and abusing the concept of the Third World: Geopolitics and the comparative political study of development and underdevelopment', *Third World Quarterly* 25:1 (2004), pp. 41–53.

Reno, Josh, 'September 11 attacks (aftermath)', in *Encyclopedia of Consumption and Waste: The social science of garbage*, ed. by Carl A. Zimring and William L. Rathje (Sage Publications, 2012).

Reyes, Alfonso, 'Notas sobre la inteligencia americana', in *Latinoamérica: Cuadernos de cultura latinoamericana*, 15 (1976 [1936]), pp. 5–12.

Rivera Cusicanqui, Silvia, 'Ch'ixinakax utxiwa: A reflection on the practices and discourses of decolonization', *South Atlantic Quarterly* 111:1 (2012), pp. 95–109.

Rockström, Johan, Will L. Steffen, Kevin Noone, Åsa Persson, F. Stuart Chapin III, Eric Lambin, Timothy M. Lenton et al., 'Planetary boundaries: Exploring the safe operating space for humanity', *Ecology and Society* 14:2 (2009), article 32, <https://www.ecologyandsociety.org/vol14/iss2/art32/> [accessed 28 December 2022].

Rohrig, Brian, 'Smartphones', *ChemMatters* 12 (2015).

Scandura, Jani, *Down in the Dumps: Place, Modernity, American Depression* (Duke University Press, 2008).

Schaffer, Guy, 'Camp', in *Discard Studies Compendium*, 2010, <https://discardstudies.com/discard-studies-compendium/#Camp> [accessed 15 June 2021].

Scheel, David, Stephanie Chancellor, Martin Hing, Matthew Lawrence, Stefan Linquist & Peter Godfrey-Smith, 'A second site occupied by Octopus tetricus at high densities, with notes on their ecology and behavior', *Marine and Freshwater Behaviour and Physiology* 50:4 (2017), pp. 285–91.

Schmelzer, Matthias, Andrea Vetter & Aaron Vansintjan, *The Future Is Degrowth: A guide to a world beyond capitalism* (Verso Books, 2022).

Schnapp, Alain, *Une histoire universelle des ruines* (Seuil, 2020).

Schwartz, Roy et al., 'Green AI', *Communications of the ACM* 63:12 (2020), pp. 54–63.

Shanks, Michael, David Platt & William L. Rathje, 'The perfume of garbage: Modernity and the archaeological', *Modernism/Modernity* 11 (2004), 61–83.

Sharpe, Christina, *In the Wake: On Blackness and being* (Duke University Press, 2016).

Silva, Cristian, 'The interstitial spaces of urban sprawl: Unpacking the marginal suburban geography of Santiago de Chile', in *Creative Spaces: Urban culture and marginality in Latin America*, ed. by Niall Geraghty and Adriana Laura Massidda (Institute of Latin American Studies, 2019), pp. 55–84.

Star, Susan Leigh, 'The ethnography of infrastructure', *American Behavioral Scientist* 43:3 (1999), pp. 377–91, <https://doi.org/10.1177/00027649921955326> [accessed 30 October 2022].

Sterling, Bruce, 'The life and death of media', in *Sound Unbound: Sampling digital music and culture*, ed. by Paul D. Miller (MIT Press, 2008), pp. 73–82.

Stoler, Ann Laura, ed., *Imperial Debris: On ruins and ruination* (Duke University Press, 2013).

Strubell, Emma, Ananya Ganesh & Andrew McCallum, 'Energy and policy considerations for deep learning in NLP', in *Proceedings of the 57th Annual Meeting of the Association for Computational Linguistics* (Florence, Italy, 2019), pp. 3645–50, <http://arxiv.org/abs/1906.02243> [accessed 30 December 2022].

Su, Lian Jye, *Environmentally Sustainable 5G Deployment: Energy consumption analysis and best practices* (ABI Research, 2020).

Sullivan, Martin J. P. et al., 'Long-term thermal sensitivity of Earth's tropical forests', *Science* 368 (2020), 869–74.

Taffel, Sy, 'AirPods and the earth: Digital technologies, planned obsolescence and the Capitalocene', *Environment and Planning E: Nature and Space*, January 2022, <https://doi.org/10.1177/25148486221076136> [accessed 30 October 2022].

Taffel, Sy, 'Data and oil: Metaphor, materiality and metabolic rifts', *New Media & Society*, June 2021, <https://doi.org/10.1177/14614448211017887> [accessed 30 October 2022].

Thieme, Tatiana, Eszter Krasznai Kovacs & Kavita Ramakrishnan, 'Refugees as new Europeans, and the fragile line between crisis and solidarity', *Journal of the British Academy* 8 (2020), pp. 19–25.

Thompson, Michael, *Rubbish Theory: The creation and destruction of value* (Oxford University Press, 1979).

Thylstrup, Nanna Bonde, 'Data out of place: Toxic traces and the politics of recycling', *Big Data & Society* 6:2 (2019), pp. 1–2.

Treanor, Jill, 'Half of world's wealth now in hands of 1% of population', *The Guardian*, 13 October 2015, <https://www.theguardian.com/money/2015/oct/13/half-world-wealth-in-hands-population-inequality-report> [accessed 20 January 2022].

Tsing, Anna et al. (eds.), *Arts of Living on a Damaged Planet: Ghosts and monsters of the Anthropocene* (University of Minnesota Press, 2017).

Vergès, Françoise, 'Capitalocene, waste, race, and gender', *e-flux* 100 (2019), <https://www.e-flux.com/journal/100/269165/capitalocene-waste-race-and-gender> [accessed 15 June 2021].

Villaseñor, Nélida R. et al., 'Vacant lands as refuges for native birds: An opportunity for biodiversity conservation in cities', *Urban Forestry & Urban Greening* 49 (2020), 126632.

Vincent, James, 'Bitcoin consumes more energy than Switzerland, according to new estimate', *The Verge*, 4 July 2019 <https://www.theverge.com/2019/7/4/20682109/bitcoin-energy-consumption-annual-calculation-cambridge-index-cbeci-country-comparison> [accessed 26 October 2022].

Vindrola-Padrós, Bruno, *The Early Neolithic Broken World: The role of pottery breakage in central and southeastern Europe* (unpublished doctoral thesis, UCL, 2020).

Walters, Gretchen et al., 'Deciphering African tropical forest dynamics in the Anthropocene: How social and historical sciences can elucidate forest cover change and inform forest management', *Anthropocene* 27 (2019), article 100214.

Wang, Z. Yan, Melissa R. Pergande, Clifton W. Ragsdale & Stephanie M. Cologna, 'Steroid hormones of the octopus self-destruct system', *Current Biology* 32:11 (2022), pp. 2572–9.e4, <https://doi.org/10.1016/j.cub.2022.04.043> [accessed 3 January 2023].

Wang, Z. Yan & Clifton W. Ragsdale, 'Multiple optic gland signaling pathways implicated in octopus maternal behaviors and death', *Journal of Experimental Biology* 221:19 (2018), jeb185751 <https://doi.org/10.1242/jeb.185751> [accessed 27 Oct 2022].

Weiser, Mark, 'The computer for the 21st century', *Scientific American* 265:3 (1991), pp. 94–104.
Yusoff, Kathryn, *A Billion Black Anthropocenes or None* (University of Minnesota Press, 2018).
Zero Waste International Alliance, 'Zero waste definition', 2018, <https://zwia.org/zero-waste-definition/> [accessed 29 October 2022].
Zografos, Stamatis, *Architecture and Fire: A psychoanalytic approach to conservation* (UCL Press, 2019).

Milton Keynes UK
Ingram Content Group UK Ltd.
UKHW051407200524
442975UK00049B/1457